THE
PICTORIAL HISTORY
OF
AMERICAN AIRCRAFT

THE PICTORIAL HISTORY

OF

AMERICAN AIRCRAFT

Bill Yenne

NEW YORK
A Bison Book

TABLE OF CONTENTS

Copyright © 1988 by Bison Books Corp

First published in USA 1988
by Exeter Books
Distributed by Bookthrift
Exeter is a trademark of Bookthrift Marketing, Inc.
Bookthrift is a registered trademark of Bookthrift
Marketing, Inc.
New York, New York

ISBN 0-7917-0208-1

Printed in Spain

Page 1: This World War II photograph depicts a ground crew inspecting the landing gear of one of America's mightiest fighters, the Lockheed P-38 Lightning. The Lightning performed in all theaters of World War II, and German pilots expressed the prevailing Axis sentiment towards the plane in calling the P-38 'the Fork-Tailed Devil.'

Pages 2-3: Suffused with an eerie light befitting the 'Blackbird's' unusual contours, this in-hangar photo catches the SR-71 in a moment of stillness. This spy plane routinely flies at speeds in excess of Mach 3.

Page 6: Would-be WAFs (women pilots) of the USAAF (circa 1942) gather around a North American AT-6 Texan advanced trainer to listen to an old hand describe the joys and dangers of solo flight. During World War II, much of the transporting of military aircraft within the continental United States was done by WAFs.

Edited by Pamela Berkman and John Kirk

Designed by Bill Yenne

Captioned by Timothy Jacobs

Introduction

The airplane itself was born in the United States with the first flight of a manned heavier-than-air craft at Kitty Hawk, North Carolina in 1903. Though the early American aircraft industry took a back seat to that of Europe in the first part of the century, a new generation of American designers emerged in the early 1920s. The companies they founded would mature over the ensuing two decades into an aircraft industry that was second to none.

In the 1930s, the American aircraft industry came of age as many of the plane-builders, whose companies had been founded on a shoestring in the years before, finally matured. Boeing, Douglas and Lockheed became household words as their products flowed from the factory door to the airways of the world. The major airlines of the United States—American, National, Pan American and Transcontinental & Western Air (TWA)—also matured during this period as their route maps spread across the continent, binding its farthest reaches to one another and to the world.

World War II saw the American aircraft industry aspire to an unprecedented performance, both in the number of aircraft produced and in the level of technological development achieved. In the space of five years nearly a quarter of a million aircraft rolled off American assembly lines and into the armed services of the United States and its allies. This amazing production record is made more so when one realizes that the same industry that was building open-cockpit biplanes in 1941 was producing jets by 1945.

After the war American aircraft evolved nearly as fast as they had during the war. Two years after VJ day, in 1947, the Bell X-1 was used to break the sound barrier for the first time, and within a decade, aircraft were being built that could operate routinely in a Mach 2 environment. On the commercial side, American aircraft have held the undisputed leading role since the second World War. The Lockheed Constellations, Douglas DC-6 and DC-7 dominated the skies until the advent of practical jetliners in the mid-1950s. The first generation of American jetliners—the Boeing 707 and 727, and the Douglas DC-8 and DC-9—made air travel by jet routine within a decade. In the early 1970s, a triumvirate of huge jetliners—the Boeing 747, Douglas DC-10 and Lockheed L-1011—helped define the concept of the 'wide bodied jumbo jet' and soon these aircraft served nearly every major airline in the world.

Though not without important competition abroad, the American industry and American aircraft are still predominant in the worlds' skyways. At every major airport in the world is at least one line of American-built light planes or jetliners from the factories of California or Seattle. NATO's air forces all fly aircraft of American design, whether they be C-130 Hercules transports built by Lockheed of Georgia or F-16 Falcons from the drafting boards of General Dynamics in Fort Worth, Texas. Even France, with its strong national aerospace industry, flies Boeing refueling aircraft to support its air force and Vought Crusaders from its Navy's aircraft carriers.

American aircraft and aviators have always been on the leading edge. From the Wrights themselves to Admiral Byrd and his conquest of the South Pole, to Lindbergh's solo Atlantic Flight, Americans helped write aviation history. In the technology boom of the postwar years there were Americans in X-15s and SR-71s that flew higher and faster than anyone had flown before.

Our book chronicles this amazing adventure through many of the great American aircraft that made it possible. From the fragile Wright Flyers, we go full circle to the equally delicate *Voyager*, an aircraft whose challenge was no less monumental and whose success was no less triumphant.

The Formative Years

THE WRIGHT FLYERS

For centuries man had dreamed of flying—of moving through the air under his own power like a bird. Leonardo da Vinci had designed nearly-practical flying machines in the sixteenth century, while Joseph and Etienne Montgolfier made mankind's first ascent into the sky via balloon in June 1783. Throughout the nineteenth century, the art of ballooning gained followers and evolved in sophistication. Germany's Count Ferdinand von Zeppelin developed a powered airship in 1900, but all of these vehicles depended on lighter-than-air gases (either hydrogen or hot air) for their lift. Heavier-than-air flight was still just a dream, but not for want of trying. Otto Lilienthal in Germany made a number of flights between 1891 and 1896 in a series of hang gliders of his own design, but they involved climbing to a high place and gliding downward through the air. His hang gliders were kitelike in that they depended upon wind for any lift.

Meanwhile, in the United States, Professor Samuel Pierpont Langley of the Smithsonian Institution had designed and flown a model aircraft powered by a steam engine. The great inventor, Alexander Graham Bell, who witnessed Langley's experiment, was impressed and his endorsement led to President William McKinley's directing the US Army to underwrite the cost of building a manned prototype. Having made the transition from steam to gasoline engine, the full-scale Langley 'Aerodrome' was completed in 1903, but two attempts to fly the contraption resulted in failure and very nearly the death of design engineer Charles Manley, who was at the controls each time.

Langley gave up after the second try on 8 December, but less than two weeks later he was incredulous to hear that a pair of bicycle shop owners from Dayton, Ohio had supposedly made a *series* of successful heavier-than-air flights on the sand dunes of Kill Devil Hill near the improbably named Kitty Hawk peninsula in North Carolina. The two men from Ohio, Wilbur Wright, 36, and his brother Orville, 32, had shared an interest in aeronautics from their youth and had built their first unmanned glider in 1896. Between 1900 and 1902 they tested a series of manned gliders at Kitty Hawk. The Wrights

Above: Bicycle mechanics *cum* men of destiny Orville *(left)* and Wilbur Wright pose with their historic aircraft (Flyer 1) in front of its hangar at Kitty Hawk, in North Carolina. Wilbur had attempted piloting the first controlled, sustained heavier than air flight, but failed, and when Orville's turn to try piloting came four days later on 17 December 1903, he 'aced' his older brother by keeping their aircraft aloft for 12 seconds over a distance of 120 feet. *Below:* The Wright's history-making Flyer 1 in the Smithsonian.

recognized that the key to successful powered flight would be the degree of control which the pilot could exercise over his craft. They looked upon their project as an *aircraft* rather than as a modified kite or as a machine that would be controlled in the air as a boat was in the water.

The Wrights had, for example, discovered that an aircraft should not be dependent on shifts in its center of gravity for control. Rather than having a pilot lunge from right to left to steer the glider, they substituted a system of controls to adjust the wingtips of their gliders. During their successful series of glider flights in the fall of 1902, the Wrights added a movable rudder and finally decided that they had a machine that could be adapted for powered flight. The only stumbling block: They needed an engine with low enough weight and sufficient power. No such engine existed, so they built one.

The first Wright Flyer was a fabric-covered biplane with a wooden frame driven by the Wrights' own 12 hp water-cooled engine connected to two contra-rotating propellers by means of belts. Wilbur and Orville completed their Flyer during the summer of 1903 and took it to windswept Kitty Hawk in December. On the 13th, Wilbur took the first turn and succeeded only in nosing the Flyer into a dune. On 17 December 1903, however, Orville Wright took to the air for 12 seconds, covering 120 feet in the first powered flight of a manned heavier-than-air craft in history! By the end of the day, each of the brothers had made *two* successful flights, with Wilbur covering 852 feet in his last turn at the controls.

Having returned to Dayton in triumph, the Wrights shunned publicity and went to work on their Flyer 2, which was essentially the same as the Flyer except for an upgraded 16 hp engine. First flown on 23 May 1904, Flyer 2 made a number of successful flights over the next seven months. Like the Flyer, however, it showed a tendency to stall in turns, and the Wrights went back to the drawing board. The result was the larger Flyer 3 which proved to be a much more reliable airplane. In tests near Dayton, for example, the Flyer 3 was flown successfully over a distance of 34 miles, and on 5 October 1905, it set an endurance record of 38 minutes.

The next Wright aircraft would be the Wright A, which first flew on 8 May 1908. By this time, in France, Alberto Santos-Dumont and Henri Farman had both made heavier-than-air flights, but it had become axiomatic that the Wrights had invented the airplane and that the three Flyers had been the pioneer machines of a new age.

	Wright Flyer 1 (1903)	**Wright Flyer 3 (1905)**
Wing span	40'4"	40'6"
Length	21'1"	28'0"
Gross weight	750 lb	855 lb
Cruising speed	30 mph	35mph
Engine	Wright 4 cylinder	Wright 4 cylinder
Engine rating	12 hp	20 hp

Below: **One of the most famous photographs in aviation history—the first sustained, controlled heavier than air flight, with Orville Wright prone in the aircraft's crude pilot's station, and brother Wilbur caught in mid-stride, overwhelmed with awe.** *Right:* **The fourth Flyer, Wright A, in 1908.** *Below left:* **Orville and Wilbur Wright.**

THE EARLY DAYS

The Wright brothers had invented heavier-than-air flight, but they were technicians, not entrepreneurs, and they were quickly oveshadowed by a new breed of aviation pioneer.

Glenn Hammond Curtiss of Hammondsport, New York was a natural mechanic with an avid interest in aeronautics, but beyond this, he bore little similarity to the shy and retiring Wrights. While the Wrights came to aircraft from bicycles, Curtiss had cut his teeth on motorcycles. It was a perfect allegory for the differences in their personalities.

Amid the publicity following the success of the Wright Flyers, there was a predictable ground swell of interest in aircraft development. One of the more serious efforts was the Aerial Experiment Association (AEA) founded and financed by a consortium that included the great inventor Dr Alexander Graham Bell. It hired Curtiss to supervise the design and flight testing of AEA aircraft and engines. The first prototype, the *Red Arrow*, flew on 12 March 1908, but crashed on its second flight. Another AEA aircraft was completed in

1908, but it was lost after just a few wobbly test flights. The third prototype, the *June Bug*, was technically more successful. Although the *June Bug* flew for two miles, it eventually flew straight into a lawsuit from the Wrights for patent infringement. The court ruled against Curtiss, but he was undeterred in his efforts to build aircraft.

In 1909 he piloted his *Golden Flyer* to a world speed record at Rheims, France. By 1913, the 35-year-old Curtiss had designed or helped to design nearly three dozen aircraft types and was the largest aircraft builder in the United States. His company even went on to swallow the Wrights' in 1929 (Wilbur died in 1912 and Orville sold out in 1915), and to hold its place as a major American aircraft builder through World War II.

Curtiss is best remembered, however, as the originator of the first important *mass-produced* American aircraft. The famous Curtiss JN series—known universally as the Jennys—originated in 1914 with the Model J. Like the Curtiss Models G and H of the preceding year, the Model J was a tractor

Above: A Curtiss Model J above Keuka Lake in 1915. The model J served as a prototype for the famous Curtiss JN Models—or 'Jennys,' as they were known. One of the airplane's early roles was as an aerial arena—for the type of performance that usually occurred only in a circus tent. The performers in such spectacles billed themselves as 'dare devils,' and were often as foolish as that appellation implies—as we can see in the photo at *upper right*, featuring two Jennies and a trapeze acrobatty (sic).

biplane, which meant that the propeller pulled rather than pushed the aircraft. While this arrangement soon became standard on most aircraft, it was rare prior to 1913. The Wright Flyers had pusher props, as did nearly all of the early Curtiss airplanes.

While the Models G and H had been designed by the staff of the Curtiss works at Hammondsport, New York, the remarkably clean lines of the Model J were due to the work of B Douglas Thomas, whom Glenn Curtiss had hired away from Sopwith Aviation in England. The first Model J rolled out on 12 March 1914 and was delivered to the US Army Signal Corps on 28 July. In September Lt Lewis Goodier established a record 1000-feet-per-minute climb in the new ship. A second Model J was delivered on 13 October. Both aircraft crashed the following year and plans for a slightly smaller J-2 were canceled in favor of the larger Model N. Only a single Model N is recorded to have been produced, and it was delivered to the Signal Corps on 11 December 1914.

The second Curtiss Model J (Army serial number 30) served as the prototype for the JN series in 1915 and as such became the first 'Jenny.' One production JN-1 was produced in 1914 as a gunnery trainer for the US Navy and was followed by a pair of JN-1S single-float seaplanes that also served the Navy.

A total of eight JN-2s were in turn delivered to the Army in time to wind up in New Mexico in March 1915 under the command of Major Benny Foulois as part of General John J Pershing's expeditionary force sent in pursuit of the Mexican bandit Pancho Villa. Foulois, who went on to serve as Chief of the US Army Air Corps from 1931 to 1935, became the first Army airman to command aircraft in combat and the JN-2s were the first American warplanes to see action.

The early Jennys proved to be less than a match for the task because their Curtiss OXX engines could not function properly in the high altitude environment of the Sonora Desert Plateau country. In the meantime, the larger but more powerful JN-3 had been introduced and the Army undertook to retrofit the JN-2s in the field with bigger engines in an effort to bring them up to the JN-3 standard. The results were not particularly successful; the Jennys were still underpowered and unsuited to the harsh high desert.

Later in 1916, however, the Army began to take delivery of the first of the JN-4 series, the definitive Jenny. An unprecedented total of 65 JN-4s were delivered with 90 hp Curtiss OX-5 engines, followed by a pair of JN-4As for the Navy and an incredible 350 JN-4As for the Army. As many as 710 JN-4B and JN-4C Jennys followed as the United States joined the Western Allies in World War I after April 1917.

The Jenny became the standard US Army Signal Corps trainer and a number of JN-4Cs were built under license in Canada by Canuck to serve as trainers for the British Royal Flying Corps training centers north of the border.

Well over three thousand JN-4Ds were built as the United States geared up for war, making it the standard production Jenny. The JN-4H 'Hisso-Jenny' series was basically a JN-4D series powered by Wright Hispano 150 hp or 180 hp engines. Various conversions were made to the JN-4D and JN-4H types, including the aircraft that became the JN-5 bombing trainer. The JN-6 was a series of more than a thousand specialized factory-built training types, including the JN-6H, which was a production version of the JN-4HB bombing

Below: Pilot controls for the Jenny were usually in the rear cockpit—which is a relief in that the fellow astride the tail is just a passenger! Actually, pilots could be zany, too.

trainer conversion. Other JN-6 Jennys included the JN-6HG gunnery trainer, the JN-6HO observation trainer, and the JN-6HP pursuit trainer.

By the time the war ended in 1918, the Curtiss Jenny had proven itself as a first rate pilot trainer and as one of the world's most reliable airplanes. Furthermore, over 7000 (sources vary) Jennys had been produced between 1915 and 1918, more than any other American-designed aircraft in history, and more than would be produced of any American type until World War II.

The second important name to follow those of Glenn Curtiss and the Wrights into the who's who of American aviation was Glenn Luther Martin, an automobile dealer from Santa Ana, California. Glenn Martin got into flying in 1909 by building a copy of the Glenn Curtiss *June Bug*, and founded his own aircraft company in Los Angeles three years later. In 1914, he hired Grover Loening, an aeronautical engineer, who would one day preside over his own firm. Loening was able to convince the US Army that the Martin designs were better than those of many Wright and Curtiss aircraft that were currently in service and won a contract for 17 Martin Model TTs that established the company.

In 1915, Martin sold out to the same consortium that had bought Orville Wright's patents, and the Wright-Martin Company was formed. After World War I, the firm was liquidated, with the Martin component winding up in Baltimore, Maryland, where it later established itself as an important builder of military aircraft as well as transoceanic commercial flying boats.

Another early customer for Glenn Martin's flying boats had been a Seattle lumber company owner named William Edward Boeing. He had flown for the first time on Independence Day in 1914 as a passenger in a Curtiss seaplane. Enraptured by flying, like so many of his contemporaries, Boeing decided to become a planemaker. He enrolled in Martin's California flying school and

Above: **Bill Boeing (center) readies himself to board his Pacific Aero Products Model C floatplane for the first international air mail run (Seattle to Vancouver) in 1919.** *Below:* **The launching of the Boeing & Westervelt *Bluebill*. See the text on page 18.**

flew home in October 1915 in a seaplane he purchased from Martin for ten thousand dollars.

Just as the Curtiss *June Bug* had been copied as Glenn Martin's first airplane, Bill Boeing used Martin's TT as the basis for his own first design. Working with his partner, navy commander Conrad Westervelt, Boeing went to work on the B&W Model 1 in a boathouse on Seattle's Lake Union. By 29 June 1916, the first of two Model 1s, the *Bluebill*, was ready to fly. Herb Munter, the test pilot that Boeing had hired for the first flight, was late to arrive, so Boeing himself climbed aboard and took his bird aloft.

When Boeing landed, a chagrined Herb Munter was the first to greet him. When he was asked how the flight had gone, Boeing told his employees on the Lake Union dockside that they were now in the airplane business. Three weeks later, Boeing founded Pacific Aero Products, a firm which eventually evolved into the Boeing Airplane Company.

In 1915, as Glenn Martin was gearing up to produce flying boats for the Navy, he hired a young recent graduate of the Massachusetts Institute of Technology named Donald Wills Douglas. In January 1918, the Army issued Martin a contract for a large twin-engined bomber, and the task of designing the huge aircraft went to the 25 year old Douglas. Completed in August 1918, the Martin MB-1 did not reach large-scale production before the end of the First World War, but it gave Douglas a firm foothold on a ladder that would eventually take him to the pinnacle of success in the American aviation industry.

Having moved to Baltimore with Martin, Douglas left the firm to return to California in April 1920 and opened an office in the back room of a Los Angeles barbershop and soon found financial support in the person of David Davis, a wealthy southern Californian keen on sponsoring the first nonstop transcontinental flight. The aircraft which Douglas built, the *Cloudster*, took off from Santa Monica on 27 June 1921 but was forced down by engine failure at El Paso, Texas. Before Davis could mount a second attempt, a US Army Fokker monoplane had become the first airplane to fly coast-to-coast without a stop. Davis lost interest and abandoned the partnership. For Douglas, on the other hand, it was a matter only of a whetted appetite and he went to work on a series of *Cloudster* derivatives which he sold to the Navy and the Army. The most successful of these was the Navy's seaplane torpedo bomber, the DT-2.

In 1923, the Army purchased five DT-2s from the Navy production run for a secret project under which they were designated DWC, for Douglas World Cruiser. The project in question would be the first flight around the world by any aircraft. DWC testing began in December 1923, and on 17 March 1924 four of the aircraft took off from Clover Field adjacent to the Douglas Santa Monica factory. One of the aircraft was lost at Dutch harbor in the Aleutian Islands off Alaska and a second in the North Atlantic, but two of the original DWCs returned to Clover Field on 23 September, having circled the globe in 371 hours of actual flying time. As the builder of the DWCs, Douglas was in the world aviation spotlight and very much in demand as an aircraft builder.

A major competitor for Boeing and Douglas—Lockheed—originated in San Francisco, halfway between them on the west coast. Allan Loughead (pronounced Lockheed) was an automobile mechanic who learned to fly (like so many others) in a Glenn Curtiss biplane in 1911. Together with his brother Malcolm he built his first airplane, the Model G seaplane, in a San Francisco garage. On 15 June 1913, Loughead lifted off from San Francisco Bay on the Model G's first flight. The brothers earned a small nest egg giving airplane

Above, left to right: David Davis, sponsor of Donald Douglas' first independent design, the Cloudster (whose wooden hull is being used as a backdrop here); Donald Douglas; and Douglas' assistant, Jim Goodyear. *At right:* The Cloudster, ready to fly.

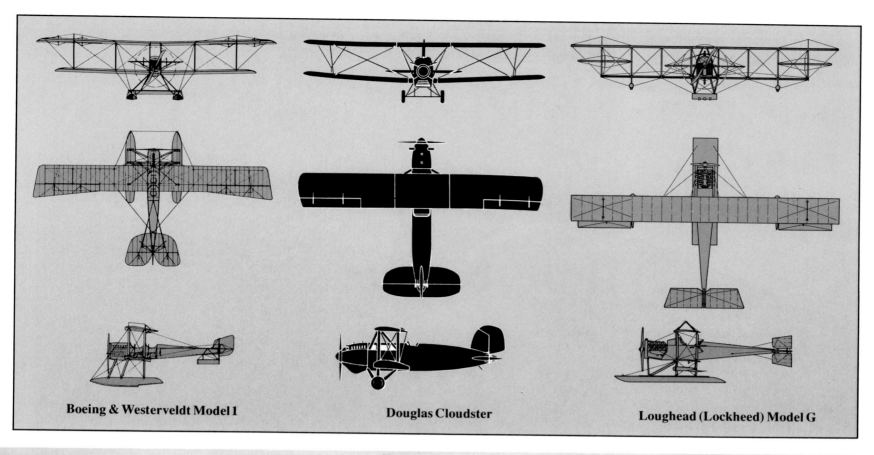

Boeing & Westerveldt Model 1 **Douglas Cloudster** **Loughead (Lockheed) Model G**

rides during the 1915 Panama Pacific Exposition in San Francisco, and in 1916 they moved their operation south to Santa Barbara.

During World War I, the Lougheads did well both with their own Model F-1 and by contract-producing Curtiss HS-2Ls, but after the war they came upon hard times. Their S-1 sport biplane failed to sell after its promising debut in 1919. Malcolm left to start his own hydraulic brake company and the Loughead Aircraft Manufacturing Company folded.

Seven years later, in December 1926, the brothers got together again, this time under the phonetic spelling of their name. The Lockheed Aircraft Company was established in Los Angeles and its first airplane, the Vega, turned out to be one of the most successful airplanes of the decade after the first one rolled out on 4 July 1927. Appearing amid the general aviation boom that followed Lindbergh's May 1927 transatlantic flight, the Vega proved to be a durable and popular airplane. In 1928, Art Goebel used his Vega to set a transcontinental speed record (23 hours, 45 minutes). A year later Amelia Earhart used hers to set a women's speed record (184.17 mph), and in 1932 she used it to become the first woman to fly solo across the Atlantic. In 1931 Wiley Post flew around the world in the Vega *Winnie-Mae*, burying all previous records with a flight time of eight days and 16 hours. It had been just seven years since the Douglas World Cruisers had accomplished the same feat in 174 days.

The success of the Vega turned Lockheed into a leading builder of other fast, single-engined monoplanes. These included the Altair, Sirius (one of which was sold to Charles Lindbergh) and Orion, an important early airliner that established a routine 86-minute flight time between Los Angeles and San Francisco. In 1929, Lockheed was bought out by Detroit Aircraft Company

The Founding Airplanes of the Great Dynasties

Specifications	AEA/Curtiss* *June Bug*	Curtiss** *Golden Flyer*	Loughead Model G	Boeing & Westervelt Model 1	Douglas Cloudster
First Flight	1908	1909	1913	1916	1921
Wing span	42′6″	28′9″	46′	52′0″	56′0″
Length	27′6″	33′6″	30′	27′6″	36′9″
Gross weight	615 lb	550 lb	2200 lb	2800 lb	9600 lb
Cruising speed	39 mph	54 mph	51 mph	70 mph	120 mph
Engine	Curtiss V-8 Cylinder	Curtiss 4 Cylinder	Curtiss 'O'	Hall-Scott A-5	Liberty 400
Engine rating	40 hp	25 hp	80 hp	125 hp	400 hp

* The first Glenn Martin airplane was actually a 1909 *copy* of the *June Bug*.
** Though Glenn Curtiss collaborated on the Aerial Experiment Association *June Bug*, the *Golden Flyer* was the first *true* Curtiss aiplane.

Above left: The more extroverted of the brothers Loughead (pronounced 'Lockheed'), Allan Loughead explains the Loughead Model G to a young lady. *Below left:* With two passengers on board, Allan Loughead brings the Model G in for a safe landing on San Francisco Bay during the 1915 Panama Pacific Exhibition. Passengers were thrilled with the novelty of seeing their day-to-day world from *up there*. *Below:* The Douglas World Cruiser. World Cruisers were the first airplanes to circle the globe (see text, page 18).

against the wishes of Allan Loughead, and three years later, despite the success of the Vega and Orion, the weight of the Great Depression forced the company out of business in 1932. It was a short-lived demise, however.

Other early American aircraft companies that appeared on the scene after World War I were founded by men whose names will be forever associated with American aviation history, even though in some cases their actual tenure with these companies was short lived. They included Walter Beech, Larry Bell, Clyde Cessna, Walter Fairchild, Edson Gallaudet, Matty Laird, Claude Ryan, Lloyd Stearman and Chance Vought, not to mention Buck Weaver, of Weaver Aircraft Co (WACO). The company that Claude Ryan founded in 1921 is notable for having produced the NYP, the Wright Whirlwind-powered monoplane nicknamed *Spirit of St Louis* with which Charles Lindbergh made his historic solo Atlantic crossing on 20-21 May 1927.

Another man whose name emerged during this period was John K 'Jack' Northrop. One of America's most important aircraft designers, his career included a number of aircraft companies, including several that bore his name. Jack Northrop started with the Loughead brothers in Santa Barbara in 1916 at age 20 and moved to Douglas in Santa Monica when Loughead went out of business in 1921. He returned to help found Lockheed Aircraft Company in 1926, where he is credited with the design of the Vega. At the same time he helped design the Ryan M-2 mail plane, a forerunner of the *Spirit of St Louis*. He went on to start the first Northrop Aircraft Company, which rolled out the Northrop Alpha, a fast low-wing monoplane, in 1930. Jack Northrop went on to produce a series of successors to the Alpha—including the predictably named Beta and Gamma—before his original Northrop company was absorbed by Douglas in 1938.

Above: Allan Loughead (at photo left) and his draftsman, the young John Northrop. *At top right:* Charles Lindbergh, the first to solo nonstop across the Atlantic, and, *at top extreme right,* the plane in which he did it, a modified Ryan NYP. *At right:* An airmail service Waco 10. Buck Weaver was gone, and 'Waco' had become the Advance Aircraft Company. The Company's planes, still known as 'Wacos,' were in demand up to World War II.

THE FIRST AIRLINERS

Commercial aviation was born the first time someone paid someone else to take him for an airplane ride, and experiments in scheduled service began in the United States as early as 1914: but it was not until after the first World War that commercial aviation was taken seriously as an alternative to ground transportation. The first airlines, St Petersburg-Tampa Airboat (1914) and Aeromarine Sightseeing & Navigation (1919) were born in Florida as tourist carriers, but the first real boon to commercial aviation came with the passage of the Kelly Air Mail Act of February 1925 that allowed for commercial, rather than government, air mail carriers. Many of the airlines bidding on the Contract Air Mail (CAM) routes parceled out by the Post Office Department were formed specially for this purpose, so the net result of the Kelly Act was none other than the genesis of the American commercial airline system as we know it.

CAM-1 (New York to Boston) went to Colonial Air Lines; CAM-2 (Chicago to St Louis) went to Robertson Aircraft Corporation; CAM-3 (Chicago to Dallas) went to National Air Transport; CAM-4 (Los Angeles to Salt Lake City) went to Western Air Express; CAM-5 (Salt Lake City to Seattle) went to Varney

Air Lines; both CAM-6 and CAM-7 (out of Detroit) went to Henry Ford's Ford Air Transport; CAM-8 (Los Angeles to Seattle) went to Pacific Air Transport; CAM-9 (Chicago to Minneapolis) went to Northwest Airways; CAM-10 (Atlanta to Jacksonville) went to Florida Airways; CAM-11 (Cleveland to Pittsburgh) went to Pennsylvania Central Airlines; and finally, CAM-12 (Pueblo to Cheyenne) went to Western Air Express.

It was out of these early pioneers that many of today's important airlines were born. National Air Transport, Varney Speed Lanes (formerly Varney Air Lines) and Pacific Air Transport all eventually became part of today's United Air Lines, while TWA evolved out of Transcontinental Air Transport and Western Air Express. Northwest, of course, remains Northwest, and Florida Airways evolved into Pan American. United Air Lines, the first really big American airline, evolved out of Bill Boeing's Boeing Air Transport, an airline that he formed in conjunction with his development of the Boeing Model 40 twin-engined and Model 80 tri-motored airliners.

In the 1920s, it seemed only natural that aircraft manufacturers should be involved in the development of airlines. When Franklin Roosevelt was elected

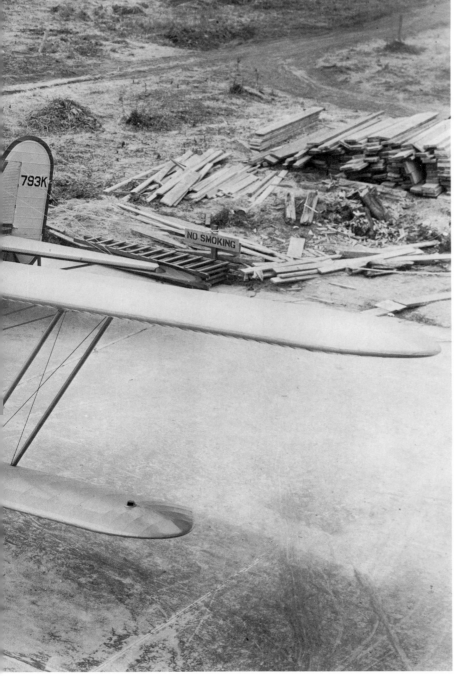

Below left: A Boeing 80-A transport at Boeing field in 1929. *Above:* The open cockpit variant, the 80-B—note the two-bladed prop on the cowl-less mid-engine of this plane, and the three-bladed side prop. Pilots preferred the open cockpit, which explains the heavy, lined leather coat modeled by the late-1920s era pilot *at right.*

in 1932, however, his administration was of the opinion that this represented a conflict of interest. As a result, Boeing was forced by law to divest itself of its interest in United Air Lines in 1934. Bill Boeing himself was so disgusted with this turn of events that he retired from the aircraft industry and lived in seclusion for the remaining two decades of his life. Both Boeing and United went on independently to become world leaders in their respective fields.

By the mid-1920s Henry Ford was one of the leading industrialists in the United States—and indeed, in the world. His Ford Motor Company, founded on a shoestring in 1903, had made him a millionaire a hundred times over and his mass-produced Model T automobiles were selling in the millions.

Fascinated with things mechanical, Ford had been interested in aviation for several years when he invested $1000 in William Bushnell 'Jacknife' Stout's Stout Metal Plane Company in 1922. Stout produced a series of all-metal aircraft culminating in the Model 2-AT Air Pullman, which was designed with the help of George Prudden. The 2-AT, a corrugated metal high wing monoplane with a single Liberty engine, was the first all-metal airliner in the United States and it was Stout's mainstay when Henry Ford bought him out in July 1925.

Ford had been impressed with Tony Fokker's F.VII three-engined monoplane transport and dreamed of producing something similar himself. He and Prudden, along with other former Stout Metal Plane engineers (which included James Smith McDonnell who later founded McDonnell Aircraft Company) experimented with several ideas, including the cumbersome 3-AT that Ford called a 'monstrosity,' before coming up with the 4-AT Trimotor. It was a 14-passenger corrugated metal aircraft with a high full-cantilever wing

of a type that was being used in Europe by Junkers, Fokker and others, but which generally had been ignored in the United States.

The Ford 4-AT Trimotor made its first flight on 11 June 1926. Nicknamed 'Tin Goose,' it sold for $42,000 and it sold fairly well, giving Fokker some stiff competition in the United States. Many airlines bought the Tin Goose and it made a major impact on the early development of the airline network throughout North America. Admiral Richard Byrd even used a 4-AT for his famous 28 November 1929 flight to the South Pole.

The 4-AT Trimotor in turn evolved into the 5-AT, a 14-passenger Trimotor powered by a trio of Pratt & Whitney Wasp radial engines delivering 450 hp. The last of the 5-ATs, which sold for $65,000, rolled off the Ford assembly line on 7 June 1933, marking a total of between 194 and 199, depending upon the source.

By this time, Henry Ford had made the decision to abandon the airplane business after his friend Harry Brooks was killed in the crash of a Ford single-engine 'Flying Flivver.' Within two years the advent of the DC-3 made practically every other airliner in the world obsolete. Nevertheless, the Trimotor's reputation was such that Ford could well have developed a follow-on that could have competed favorably with the DC-3. Whatever undeveloped potential *might have* lain among the Tin Goose's unborn descendants, the old girl herself was so durable and reliable that large numbers were still flying well into the 1960s and some examples are still flying in the 1980s.

By the early 1930s, both the airline and commercial aircraft industries in the United States were evolving rapidly. The open cockpit biplanes of a decade

continued on page 30

Above right: Henry Ford inherited this plane design when he bought out the interest of his erstwhile senior partner in Stout Metal Plane Company, William Bushnell 'Jacknife' Stout. The plane was known as the Ford 2-AT (for 'Air Transport'), and was the first all-metal airliner in the United States. Its skin was a German-invented corrugated metal called 'duraluminum.' Metal planes were something new, and were viewed somewhat askance by many aviation buffs of the 1920s.

The 2-AT evolved, under Ford's guidance (and with the help of former Stout Metal Plane Company engineers) into the unwieldy 3-AT, and then the well-known Ford Trimotor 4-AT 'Tin Goose,' which was lauded especially by passengers for its safety and reliability. The 4-AT was upgraded, and the improved version, the 5-AT (seen *below*), was the last of the Ford airplane ventures. The old 4-AT and 5-AT Tin Gooses saw much service—Admiral Richard Byrd took a 4-AT on his expedition to locate the Earth's South Pole—and some of them are flying even now, in the 1980s.

Above: A Chuck Hodgson rendering of the Lockheed Vega *Winnie Mae*, piloted by famous aeronaut Wiley Post, en route to a July 1933 around-the-world record of seven days, 18 hours and 49 minutes. This was also the first *solo* flight around the world. *Below left:* Wiley Post with *Winnie Mae*, a pair who set many speed, distance and altitude records. *At right:* A Boeing Monomail awaits its cargo with storage hatches open. *Above right:* The fastest early airliners, Lockheed Orions like these were much renowned.

Important Early Commercial Aircraft

Specifications	Ford 4-AT Trimotor	Boeing Model 80
First Flight	1926	1928
Wing span	74′	80′
Length	49′10″	54′11″
Gross weight	10,100 lb	15,276 lb
Cruising speed	107 mph	115 mph
Range	570 mi	545 mi
Engine	Wright J6 Whirlwinds (3)	Pratt & Whitney Wasps (3)
Engine rating	200 hp	425 hp

Lockheed 5 Vega	Boeing 221A Monomail	Lockheed 9D Orion	Boeing 247D	Lockheed 10 Electra	Lockheed 14 Super Electra	Boeing 307 Stratoliner
1928	1931	1931	1933	1934	1937	1939
41'	51'1.5"	42'9"	74'	55'	65'6"	107'3"
27'6"	43'5"	28'4"	51'7"	38'7"	44'4"	74'4"
4375 lb	8000 lb	5800 lb	13,650 lb	10,500 lb	15,650 lb	42,000 lb
155 mph	135 mph	205 mph	189 mph	190 mph	227 mph	215 lb
250 mi	575 mi	720 mi	745 Omi	950 mi	2060 mi	1750 mi
Pratt & Whitney Wasp	Pratt & Whitney Hornet	Pratt & Whitney Wasp	Pratt & Whitney Wasp(2)	Pratt & Whitney R985(2)	Pratt & Whitney Hornet(2)	Wright GR1820 (4)
550 hp	575 hp	550 hp	550 hp	450 hp	620hp	1100 hp

continued from page 27

before had given way to enclosed-cabin, sound-proofed aircraft that were actually *comfortable*. Air travel was finally being considered as a viable alternative to rail travel, although the railroads did not yet perceive it as a serious threat. As the 1930s began, Boeing and Lockheed emerged as the leading builders of airliners. (Considering the popularity of the Trimotors, Henry Ford could have been a strong contender and history certainly would have been different if he hadn't decided to quit the business.) Both Boeing and Lockheed built upon their early successes and unveiled revolutionary new aircraft, decidedly modern for the times. For Boeing in 1933, it was Model 247, an airplane designed to serve as the flagship on the rapidly expanding (Boeing owned) United Air Lines. Even after Boeing gave up United, the airline went ahead with the purchase of large numbers of 247s. For Lockheed in 1934, it was the Model 10 Electra, another modern liner which became an important part of the early years of Northwest. Lockheed did so well with the Model 10, with sales coming from all over the world, that the company went ahead with its Model 12 Electra Jr (1936) and Model 14 Super Electra (1937). The latter was the airplane chosen by the eccentric industrialist Howard Hughes for his record breaking flight around the world in 1938.

Even as Boeing and Lockheed were enjoying the fruits of their long years of toil in the field of commercial aircraft, an upstart from Santa Monica was waiting to upstage them. In 1932 Donald Douglas had been a reasonably successful airplane builder, but had yet to develop any commercial aircraft that had seen the kind of success enjoyed by Boeing's Model 80 or Lockheed's Orion. In August 1932, he received a letter from Jack Frye of

Above: Famous pilot Amelia Earhart set many records with her Lockheed Vega. *At right:* A Boeing Model 247-D, with Boeing Plant Number 2 in the background. *Above right:* Howard Hughes' Lockheed Model 14 Super Electra, en route to a 1938 round-the-world record of three days, 19 hours and 14 minutes. *Above far right:* A Model 10 Electra airliner.

Transcontinental & Western Air (TWA). Like most airline officials, Frye was concerned about the need for safer and more comfortable airliners. He knew that the new Boeing 247s and Lockheed Electras would fit these specifications but he was also concerned that TWA wouldn't be able to get them soon enough. He knew that Boeing would serve United first and that TWA wouldn't be able to buy any Model 247s until its competitor had all that it needed. Thus, his reason for contacting Douglas was to convince the planemaker to build a competitor to the Boeing 247. Douglas almost declined, but when he did go ahead, the result launched the most important series of propeller-driven airliners in history.

The DC-1 (Douglas, Commercial, first) made its initial flight in June 1933, shortly after that of the Boeing 247. She was larger and faster and an all-around superior airplane. After flight testing, this single prototype went into service in December. Douglas, meanwhile, was working on a production series that would be based on the DC-1, but embody a number of important improvements. Outwardly similar to the DC-1, the DC-2 had a larger passenger capacity and was capable of faster speeds and a longer range. The first of 130 commercial DC-2s went into service with TWA on 18 May 1934, just five days after its maiden flight. TWA put the first DC-2 to work on its Newark to Chicago route and broke the speed record for that run four times in the next eight days.

American Airways (later American Airlines) also became a customer for the DC-2, and like TWA, they were pleased. However, American's Chairman

Above: Passengers dining aboard a TWA DC-2. The prototype for the DC-2, the DC-1 is shown *below* at the Los Angeles Air Terminal, in 1933. *Below right:* Loading freight and supplies into a DC-2. The DC-2's 'headlights' helped distinguish it from the later DC-3.

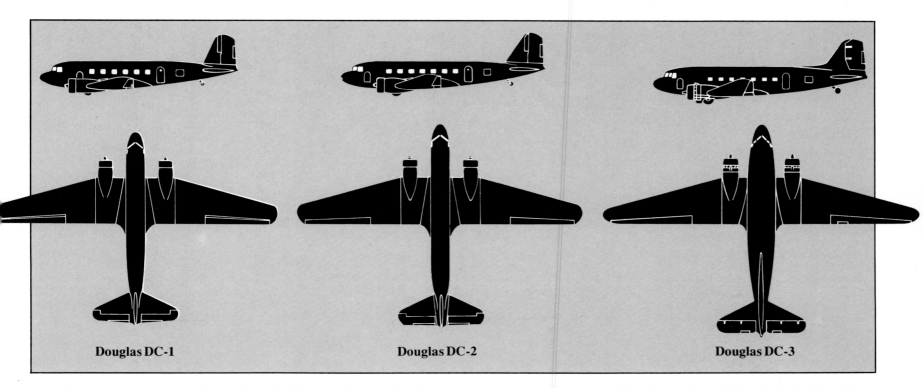

Douglas DC-1   Douglas DC-2   Douglas DC-3

Cyrus Rowlett 'CR' Smith wanted something more. He wanted a longer DC-2 with Pullman-type sleeping arrangements like the railroads offered. Again Donald Douglas was reluctant to allocate resources to development of a new aircraft type, but CR Smith's guaranteed order for 20 of them convinced Douglas. The result was the ultimate refinement of the DC-1/DC-2 design. Originally called Douglas Skysleeper Transport (DST) the new airplane was completed as the Douglas DC-3. The DC-3 Skysleeper made its first flight on 17 December 1935, the twenty-second anniversary of the Wright brothers' first flight.

The new airplane soon created such a sensation in service with American that even United lined up to buy some DC-3s. Eastern bought some two dozen as part of its Great Silver Fleet, while Braniff, Delta, Northwest, Pan American, Western and World all lined up for deliveries. The DC-3 had become the symbol of a whole new age in air travel. By 1939 it had become the single biggest factor in airline profitability as 93 percent of the world's airline passengers flew aboard the DC-3.

During World War II, thousands of DC-3s were used as military transports, with most of these serving with the USAAF under the designation C-47. Known officially as Skytrains and unofficially as Gooneybirds, the C-47s were used in every theater of the war and for every imaginable purpose, from hauling freight to pulling gliders. Under the C-53 designation they dropped American paratroopers into combat from Normandy to China, and under the name Dakota they were used in the service of British Empire air forces from England to Australia.

To say that the DC-3 eclipsed the commercial aspirations of every other twin-engined American airliner is an understatement. In the meantime, however, Boeing, Douglas and Lockheed were beginning to stir with the idea

The Douglas DC-3 model airliner was essentially an elongated DC-2 with sleeping accomodations, and is shown *above* in the colors of its first customer, American Airlines. *Below:* A DC-3 in Northwest Orient markings at the outset of WWII.

The Douglas (prewar) DC Dynasty

Specifications	DC-1	DC-2	DC-3	DC-4A[*]	DC-5
First Flight	1933	1934	1935	1942	1939
Wing span	85'	85'	94'6"	117'6"	78'
Length	60'	62'	64'6"	93'5"	62'2"
Gross weight	17,500 lb	18,560 lb	30,900 lb	82,500 lb	21,000 lb
Cruising speed	190 mph	200 mph	192 mph	207 mph	184 mph
Range	998 mi	1058 mi	1495 mi	4255 mi	1024 mi
Engine	Wright SRG1820 (2)	Wright SRG1820 (2)	Wright R1820 (2)	Pratt & Whitney R2000 (4)	Wright GR1820 (2)
Engine rating	710 hp	835 hp	1200 hp	1450 hp	1100 hp

[*] The DC-4E (Experimental) first flew in 1938. The production DC-4A was a much different airplane.

of *four*-engined super airliners. By 1939 both Boeing and Douglas had produced such an aircraft and Lockheed had one (the Constellation) on the drawing boards. Boeing came first with its Model 307 Stratoliner, which it sold to both TWA and Pan American, while Douglas undertook its DC-4 program at the behest of Boeing's old partner, United. The DC-4E (E for 'experimental') prototype was unveiled in May 1939 but it was greatly redesigned before production began.

World War II came before the DC-4 series or the Lockheed Constellation went into production, and before the Boeing 307 had any impact on the market. By the time the war ended, technology had advanced significantly and a whole new generation of airliners was born.

One class of four-engined airliners that did make a mark before the war was the big flying boats that were used to pioneer routes across the vastness of the Pacific Ocean between 1935 and 1941. The first of these was the Martin M-130 and the Sikorsky S-42, but the most well known were the huge Boeing Model 314 Clippers that were introduced in 1939. With such romantic names as *Dixie Clipper*, *Honolulu Clipper* and *Yankee Clipper*, these great ships offered the last word in luxury to travelers on both transpacific and transatlantic routes. While it had competition on the Atlantic, on the Pacific route Pan Am was king. The big Clippers flew from San Francisco to Honolulu and then on to luxury hotels that Pan Am had built in the mid-Pacific at Midway, Wake and Guam. From these exotic ports of call, Pan Am continued to Manila, Hong Kong and China itself. Inside the Boeing Model 314 was a large passenger deck with viewing windows and a formal dining room. Passenger accommodations included a bridal suite and staterooms fitted with plush davenport lounge chairs that folded into berths for a snug night's sleep.

Like many other airliners, the Clippers found their promising careers interrupted by World War II. When the war had ended and they returned from military service the Clippers found that a new generation of longer range, land-based airliners could now fly the old transoceanic routes faster and more cheaply.

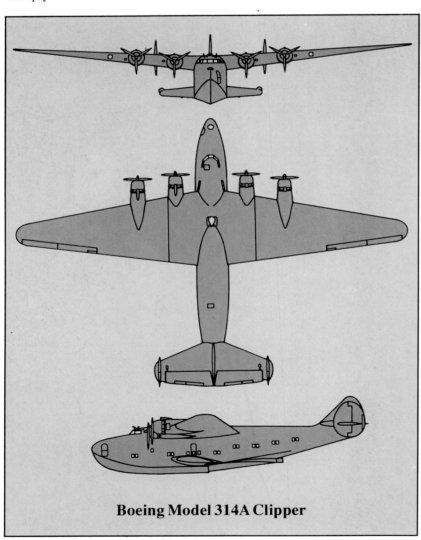

Boeing Model 314A Clipper

These pages, clockwise from immediate top right: The rather husky, and not well-received Boeing 307; the only Douglas DC-4E actually to be built had three vertical stabilizers (a configuration which was to give way to the conventional single vertical stabilizer of the regular DC-4 models); the captain and crew of a New Zealand-bound Boeing 314 A Clipper follow their passengers at an exotic stopover en route; and a very sleek-looking Douglas DC-5 high-wing transport awaits its pilot and crew in 1940. Many of these airliners saw limited military service in World War II.

The Clippers of Pan American

Specification	Sikorsky S-42	Martin M-130	Boeing 314A
First flight	1934	1934	1941
Wing Span	114′2″	130′	152′
Length	69′2″	90′11″	106′
Gross Weight	38,000 lb	52,252 lb	84,000 lb
Cruising Speed	170 mph	157 mph	199 mph
Range	1200 mi	3200 mi	5200 mi
Engine	Pratt & Whitney Hornet (4)	Pratt & Whitney Twin Wasp (4)	Wright GR2600 Twin Cyclone (4)
Engine Rating	750 hp	830 hp	1600 hp

Pan American's Clippers were flying boats which enabled the airline to give its passengers a varied, and often exotic (see previous page) service, and, given the technology of the late 1930s, were ideal for traversing large expanses of water. After World War II, however, technology had made great leaps, and the need for floatplanes—even those as incredibly luxurious as the Boeing 314—existed no longer. The new airliners could cover the same distances faster and more cheaply—and without the necessity of landing on water.

Pan American's mainstays were the Sikorsky S-42 (*at immediate right*), the Martin M-130 (*at far right*) and of course the Boeing 314—which is shown *below* in its original single vertical stabilizer configuration. The single 'tail' was replaced during test runs with a much more stable triple vertical stabilizer (see the Boeing 314 A on the previous page).

The Boeing Clipper by far outdid its companion/rivals in the genre, both in the fact that it was outfitted with such luxuries as a formal dining room and honeymoon suite, and in terms of its overall performance (see the chart *at left*).

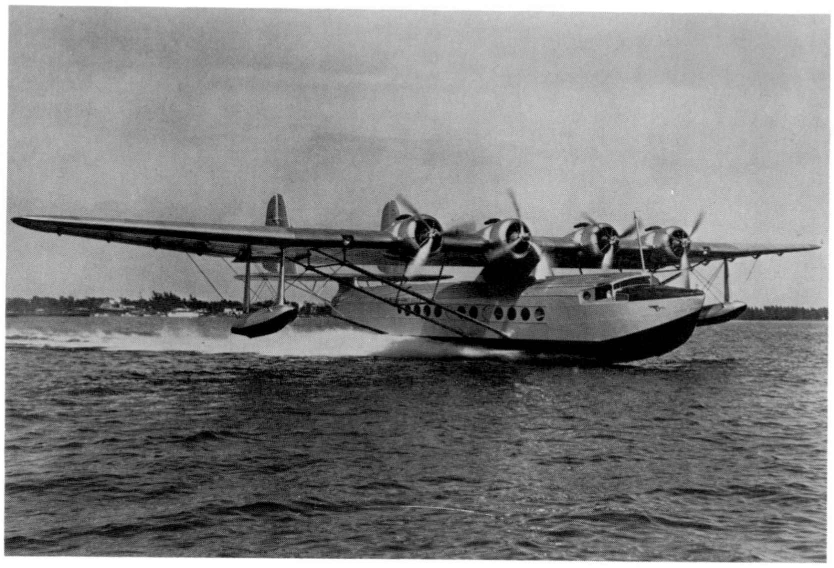

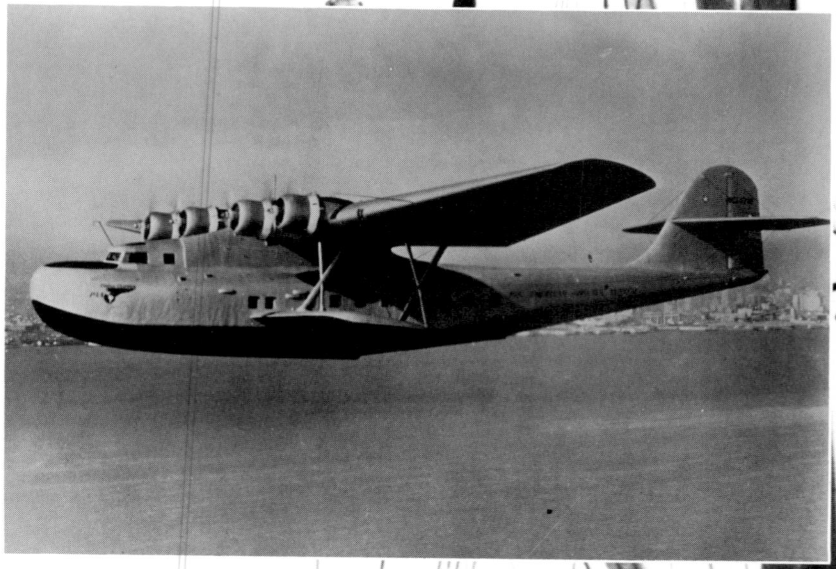

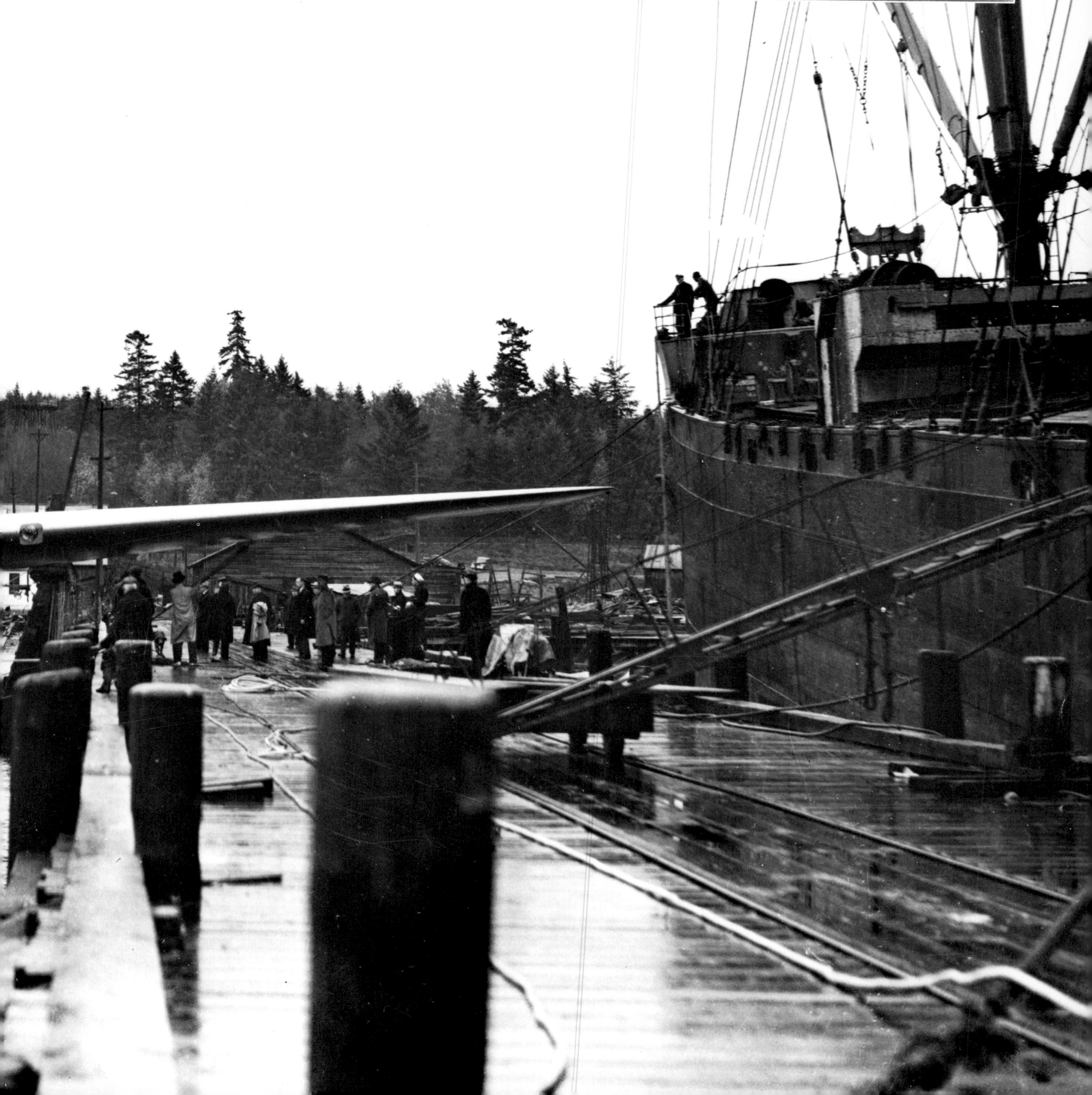

WARPLANES BETWEEN THE WARS

The United States emerged from World War I without any domestically built aircraft having been in combat. In the early 1920s, a major part of the US Army Air Service (Air Corps after 1926) inventory consisted of Curtiss JN-4 Jennys and British-designed and American-built de Havilland DH-4s. The Air Corps ordered a wide variety of aircraft types, but very few aircraft of each type. Even as late as 1930, an order for more than 20 airplanes of a particular type was considered good. On the US Navy side the opposite was true, but only a handful of types saw a production run in excess of 100 airplanes.

During this period, a great many manufacturers came and went, but a few established themselves as consistent suppliers. Boeing, Curtiss and Loening were the major suppliers of pursuit and attack planes, while Douglas and Thomas Morse joined Curtiss as leading builders of observation aircraft. Keystone, meanwhile, was the principal builder of bombers. Among the Navy's suppliers, both Boeing and Curtiss were again prominent, as were Martin and Vought. Both services also designed and built a number of aircraft in-house during the 1920s. The leading government manufacturing facilities were the Naval Aircraft Factory at Philadelphia and the Army Engineering Division at McCook Field near Dayton, Ohio.

In the 1930s both Boeing and Curtiss were firmly established as leaders in the manufacture of American combat aircraft. As names like Loening disappeared, new ones appeared. Some, like Lockheed, had been around for years but were now just starting to make it big, while others like Grumman on the Navy side and North American on the Army side were relative newcomers whose long and illustrious histories were still ahead of them. Both Boeing and Curtiss built aircraft for a wide variety of missions, ranging from big Navy

flying boats to speedy biplane fighters. Notable among the latter were the Boeing F4B, Boeing P-12 and the Curtiss Hawk series.

By the early 1930s, biplanes were giving way to all-metal monoplanes among every type of aircraft. This trend was certainly true of the high performance fighters of the US Army Air Corps. The first of these, the Boeing P-26 Peashooter, was also the last Air Corps fighter with an open cockpit and fixed landing gear. The Peashooter, which had the most distinctive appearance of any of its contemporaries, first flew in 1932 and served in the Air Corps until the eve of World War II. Some P-26s were transferred to the Philippine air corps and these were available at the time of the Japanese invasion in December 1941. They even managed to shoot down a couple of Japanese fighters in air-to-air combat.

Among Air Corps bombers, the name Keystone firmly dominated the field during the biplane era. Keystone, however, was a victim of changing times and the advent of the all-metal monoplane. The first generation of these new craft—the Douglas B-7, Fokker B-8 and Boeing B-9—were all open cockpit affairs. The latter, which first flew in 1931, was judged to be the best of the three and production B-9s entered service the following year. It was also in 1932 that the Martin B-10 appeared. The first enclosed cockpit Army bomber to go into production, the B-10 begat a series of successors including the B-12 and B-14. The next generation of American military aircraft—those which began to appear in 1935—would be the generation to come of age in time to help turn the tide of World War II.

Below: **Considered to be the apex of traditional biplane design, this Boeing F4B-4 Navy divebomber bears a Felix the Cat squadron logo; on this occasion, Felix's 'bag of tricks' contained a bomb.** *At right:* **A squadron of Keystone LB-7s over the Golden Gate.**

Early Military Aircraft

Specifications	Keystone LB-7 light bomber	Boeing P-12	Curtiss P-6 Hawk	Boeing F4B	Boeing P-26 Peashooter
First Flight	1928	1931	1932	1932	1932
Wing span	75'	30'	31'6"	30'	28'
Length	43'5"	20'1"	23'2"	20'5"	23'7"
Gross weight	12,903 lb	2629 lb	3392 lb	2898 lb	2995 lb
Cruising speed	95 mph	150 mph	198 mph	160 mph	200 mph
Range	432 mi	675 mi	285 mi	585 mi	635 mi
Engine	Pratt & Whitney Hornet (2)	Pratt & Whitney Wasp (1)	Curtiss Conqueror (1)	Pratt & Whitney Wasp (1)	Pratt & Whitney Wasp (1)
Engine rating	525 hp	460 hp	700 hp	550 hp	600 hp

Above: A 'stack' formation of Boeing P-26A 'Peashooters.' The Peashooter was the US Army's first monoplane fighter, and also its first all-metal airplane. *At right:* Air Corps Captain Ira Eaker stands next to his steed, a speedy Boeing P-12 biplane fighter in this 1929 photo. During World War II, as *General* Eaker, he commanded the USAAF Eighth Air Force.

Boeing P-12   **Boeing P-26**

CAPTAIN EAKER
WITH P-12
2327-B 2-26-29

Part Two

The War Years

USAAF BOMBERS OF WORLD WAR II

By the late 1930s, as war clouds began to gather over Europe, Germany had become the world leader—both qualitatively and quantitatively—in military aircraft. The United States at that time ranked well behind not only Germany but Britain and Japan. In the area of four-engined bombers the United States held the lead, but that was only because the field hadn't been developed. Some experimental work had been done in most countries but only the United States and Britain would take the concept seriously before the war, and the United States had about a two year lead.

The Air Corps began studying the problem of delivering a ton of bombs over a 5000 mile range with its Project A between July 1933 and April 1934. Project A in turn led to a request for proposals under the designation Experimental Bomber, Long Range (XBLR). Though both Boeing and Martin submitted ideas, only the Boeing SBLR-1 (delivered as XB-15) was ever

Note: The US Army Air Corps (USAAC) became the US Army Air Forces (USAAF) on 20 June 1941. The USAAF in turn became the completely independent US Air Force (USAF) on 18 September 1947.

built. Before this huge experimental aircraft was complete, however, Boeing found itself squaring off against Martin and Douglas over a more lucrative contract to build a series of production aircraft.

The Air Corps' request called for this airplane to be the largest and most capable production series bomber that it had ever ordered. The request specified that it be 'multiengined.' In the past this had always meant *two* engines, and so the Martin and Douglas proposals had two. Boeing's, however, had four.

Both the Boeing Model 299 and Douglas Model DB-1 were delivered to the Air Corps in prototype form in 1935. They were, in turn, ordered into production as the B-17 and B-18, respectively. The Douglas B-18 Bolo went on to a much overlooked role during World War II with the USAAF Antisubmarine Command, while the Boeing B-17 Flying Fortress began a career as one of the half dozen greatest aircraft in history!

By the time the United States entered World War II in December 1941, the B-17 had been in squadron service for more than a year, but in relatively small numbers. Those B-17s that were in the Philippines at the time counterattacked in a valiant, but doomed, defense. Boeing quickly increased production of the B-17, incorporating more defensive armament into the

Above: The XB-17, the prototype for one of the most successful bombers ever flown, at Boeing Plant Number 1, in Seattle. *Below:* An excellent view of the ultimate B-17, a B-17G, in action over Germany in 1944. This photo was taken from the waistgunner's position of a neighboring B-17G. The drab coloration shown here was replaced with a natural aluminum finish in the last years of WWII, and the vast numbers of B-17s that flew bombing runs over Germany then were termed, en masse, 'Aluminum Overcast.'

B-17E and B-17F models, which were introduced in 1942. For its part, the USAAF established its Eighth Air Force, an organization that would be based in England for the purpose of attacking Nazi-occupied Europe with heavy bombers, the most important of which would be the B-17.

In the first Eighth Air Force heavy bomber raid against Europe, a dozen B-17s struck the rail yards at Rouen, France on 17 August 1942. From that point forward, the Eighth Air Force gradually and steadily increased its pressure against the Germans, until the vast thousand-plane armadas of B-17s came to be referred to as the 'aluminum overcast.'

In 1943, the USAAF activated its Fifteenth Air Force, another heavy bomber air force designed to strike at Germany's war-making ability, in the Mediterranean. Also in 1943 Boeing introduced the B-17G, the most heavily armed of the Flying Fortresses, and the subtype of which the most aircraft were built. Though the 'Forts' served with the USAAF in every theater of the war, it was with the Eighth and Fifteenth in Europe that the aircraft made its biggest impact and its most important contribution to final victory.

A second important USAAF heavy bomber in World War II was the Consolidated B-24 Liberator. The evolution of the Liberator began in January 1939 when USAAF Commanding General Henry H 'Hap' Arnold asked the Consolidated Aircraft Company to design a 300 mph bomber with a 3000 mile range. Arnold already was planning for a huge superbomber—one which would eventually become the B-29—but in the meantime, he wanted a bomber that was incrementally better than the B-17 but that didn't push the limits of untried technology as far as the superbomber would. He knew that if there were a war, the USAAF would need all the planes it could get, as fast as it could get them. Parallel production of the B-17 and another heavy bomber while the USAAF was waiting for the superbomber to develop made sense on paper and it would soon prove to make even more sense in reality.

The USAAF accepted Consolidated's Model 32 proposal on 30 March 1939 and asked the company to go ahead with a prototype under the designation XB-24. For its length, the Model 32 had tremendous fuselage *volume*, a factor

continued on page 52

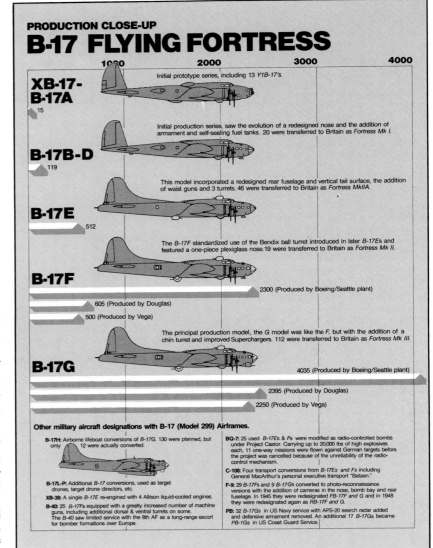

PRODUCTION CLOSE-UP
B-17 FLYING FORTRESS

Below: **B-17Gs in the final assembly stage at Boeing's Plant Number 2 in the thick of World War II. At peak production, more than 500 B-17Gs rolled off the assembly line per month.** *At right:* **A fighter escort's eye view of an Eighth Air Force B-17G 'Flying Fortress' on a bombing run over Germany in World War II.**

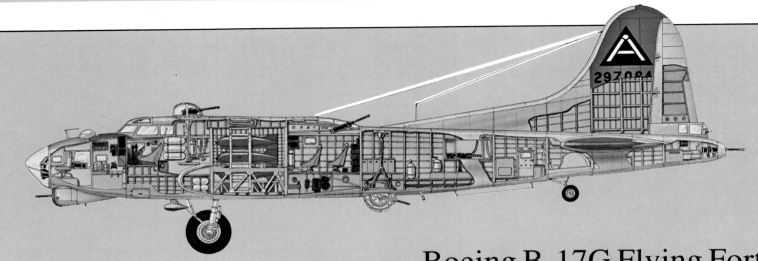

Boeing B-17G Flying Fortress

At left: A B-17G delivering its 17,600 pounds of bombs. *Above:* A cutaway view of an Eighth Air Force (1st Bomb Wing, 91st Bomb Group) B-17G. The B-17G was defensively armed with no less than 13 .50 caliber machine guns, which fired ketchup bottle sized cartridges. The B-17 gained a reputation as an aircraft which could suffer intensive, even incredible, damage and still make it back to base. General Ira C Eaker (*see page 42*), who was in charge of developing offensive bombing tactics for the Allies in World War II, said 'The B-17, I think, was the best combat plane ever built.'

Below: A sectional view of the same B-17G Flying Fortress, showing crew stations and other design features. *At right:* The 'Aluminum Overcast' gathers for a storm over Hitler's Reich.

continued from page 48

that was to make it an extremely versatile aircraft in service. The XB-24 prototype made its first flight on 29 December 1939, one day ahead of schedule, and nearly four months after the outbreak of World War II added an air of urgency to the whole enterprise.

Through the middle of 1941, deliveries of Liberators to the RAF outpaced the trickle of B-24As into the USAAF. Because of their extremely long range, the first major deployment of USAAF Liberators was as *transports*. In September 1941 a pair of well-marked B-24As transported American envoy Averell Harriman on his harrowing mission to Moscow. The B-24D was the first large-scale production version of the Liberator and they were involved in the Halverson Project, a 1942 plan to bomb Japan from bases in China. These bombers were, however, diverted to another, perhaps more critical, long-range mission. En route to China, Colonel Halverson's Liberators received a change of orders in North Africa. On 11 June 1942 they were launched from Fayid, Egypt against the huge German oil refinery complex in Ploesti, Romania. The raid was a complete surprise, but the Liberators were not able to put much of a dent in Ploesti's refinery capacity. Another much larger B-24 raid in August 1943 was a good deal more successful despite heavy losses.

Having proved their worth as long-range heavy bombers in the Ploesti attack, B-24s joined the B-17s of the USAAF Eighth Air Force in England that were massing for the strategic air offensive against the German heartland.

While, as we've seen, the Boeing B-17 Flying Fortress was the primary USAAF heavy bomber in Europe, the Liberator played this role in the Pacific where vast distances were more easily spanned by the B-24's great range. Model 32s were also used by the Royal Australian Air Force in the Pacific.

The B-24H was a textbook example of cooperation among various primary contractors, but as famed aviation historian William Green points out, it was probably the only aircraft in history (except for subsequent Liberators) to have standard turrets produced by *four different subcontractors*. Consolidated itself built the tail turrets for all the primary contractors, while Martin built the top turret, Sperry the 'ball' turret below, and Emerson the now-institutionalized nose turret. For the 40 B-24Hs that became the RAF Coastal Command's Liberator VI, the tail turret was the four-gun Boulton Paul model indigenous to the familiar Avro Lancasters.

The definitive Liberator, however, was the B-24J, of which 6678 were delivered by five Liberator factories. The B-24J had the M-9 Norden Bombsight and the Emerson nose turret and engines that gave it more altitude by the addition of the General Electric B-22 turbo-supercharger. The same aircraft that served the USAAF as B-24J was also found in the US Navy as

Above: A B-24 Liberator during the second—and more successful—Ploesti, Romania oil refinery raid. *Below:* A B-24G, with retrofitted nose turret (which first appeared on the B-24H) in evidence. *At right:* A flight nurse christens a third Liberator for a veteran Pacific-theater crew who had their first two B-24s 'shot out from under them.'

PB4Y-1 and in the RAF as Liberator VIII. Notably, 208 of the USAAF series were converted as unarmed fuel tankers under the designation C-109. They were all part of the massive effort undertaken in 1944 to supply the Twentieth Air Force B-29s that were raiding Japan from bases in China, which were located at the end of a tenuous several-thousand-mile long supply line stretching from India across the Himalayas.

Before the war ended, the US Navy contracted with Consolidated (which merged with Vultee Aircraft in March 1943) to develop a lengthened, single-tailed version of the Liberator under the designation PB4Y-2. Before the war ended, Consolidated delivered 740 of these first cousins to the Liberator, which were known as Privateers.

Besides being the most produced bomber in history, the B-24 was an integral part of the USAAF's global effort. Barring the Douglas C-47, it is hard to think of another airplane that was used so widely by the USAAF in so many far flung locales. In September of 1944 they reached a peak of 6043 in the USAAF inventory, as compared to 4552 B-17s in the same month.

While heavy bombers garnered a great deal of the glory during World War II, light and medium bombers also shouldered a great deal of the war effort. Flying low and fast, they struck tactical targets such as bridges, shipping lines, convoys and enemy strong points. Light bombers were, on the average, barely larger than fighter bombers and carried an A for attack rather than a B for bomber designation. Important among these types early in the war were the Douglas A-20 Havoc and the Lockheed A-28/A-29 Hudson. Most of the Hudsons that were built actually served with the British Royal Air Force, while many of the Douglas bombers served the RAF under the name Boston. Later in the war, Douglas developed the idea behind its A-20 into a much more advanced attack plane which went into service as the A-26 Invader. Redesignated as B-26 between 1948 and 1967, (when it became A-26 again), the Invader had the distinction of serving not only during much of World War II but through much of the Korean and Vietnam wars as well.

Above: General Jimmy Doolittle at the controls of a B-25. As Lt Col Doolittle, he led 16 Mitchells in an attack against Tokyo in 1942. On 24 September 1929, as a lieutenant, he had piloted the first 'instrument' flight with gyrocompass equipment. *Below:* B-25s and production personnel at the North American Aviation plant in Los Angeles.

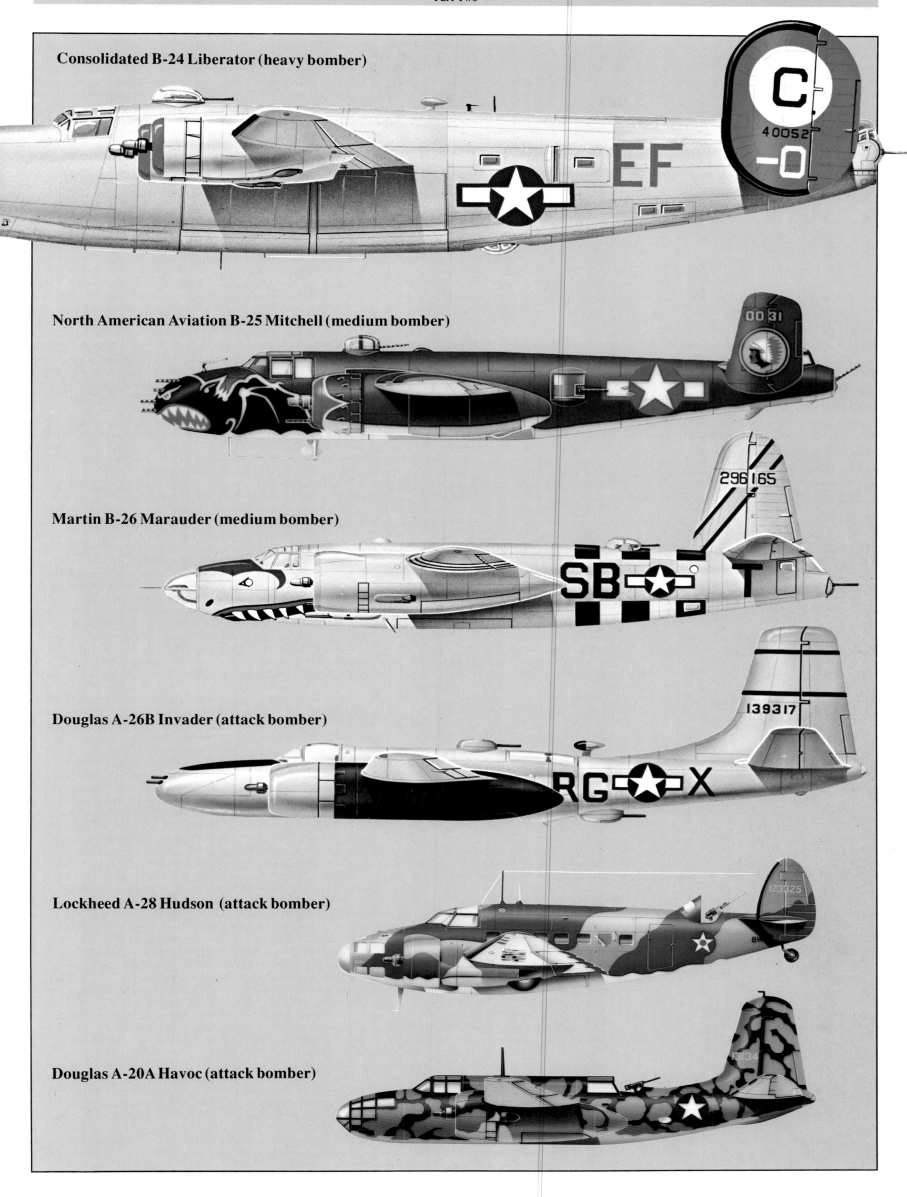

Consolidated B-24 Liberator (heavy bomber)

North American Aviation B-25 Mitchell (medium bomber)

Martin B-26 Marauder (medium bomber)

Douglas A-26B Invader (attack bomber)

Lockheed A-28 Hudson (attack bomber)

Douglas A-20A Havoc (attack bomber)

Among medium bombers, the North American B-25 Mitchell and the Martin B-26 Marauder were ubiquitous in USAAF operations throughout the world.

The B-25 was in USAAF squadron service before the United States entered World War II and entered combat in the South Pacific very early on. Its most famous combat mission came on 18 April 1942, when sixteen Mitchells, commanded by Lt Col Jimmy Doolittle, were launched from the deck of the aircraft carrier *Hornet* on a daring attack against Tokyo and other targets in Japan. The Doolittle raid did little physical damage, but it was a tremendous blow to Japanese morale and a boost to American morale at a critical juncture in the war.

Like the B-25, the Martin B-26 Marauder saw its first combat in the Pacific in 1942, but went on to serve with USAAF units throughout the world, from the jungles of southeast Asia to the beaches of Normandy. It was to be Martin's last major aircraft project for the USAAF, although a few experimental airplane projects were done for the US Air Force.

continued on page 60

Above: An early Martin B-26A in prewar markings. The B-25G and H *(at right)*, had a solid nose, while other B-25s had a glassed bombardier's station *(below and below right)*. The B-25 pictured *below* is a B-25J which was transferred to the US Navy as PBJ-1J.

USAAF Bombers of World War II

Specifications[*]	Boeing B-17 Flying Fortress	Consolidated B-24 Liberator	North American B-25 Mitchell	Martin B-26 Marauder	Boeing B-29 Superfortress
Type	Heavy	Heavy	Medium	Medium	Very Heavy
First Flight[*]	1935	1939	1940	1940	1942
Wing span	103'9"	110'	67'7"	65'	140'3"
Length	74'9"	67'2"	53'6"	58'3"	99'
Gross weight	65,500 lb	56,000 lb	27,560 lb	27,200 lb	140,000 lb
Cruising speed	160 mph	290 mph	242 mph	260 mph	220 mph
Range	2000 mi	3300 mi	1520 mi	1150 mi	5830 mi
Engine	Wright R1820 (4)	Pratt & Whitney R1830 (4)	Wright R2600 (2)	Pratt & Whitney R2800 (2)	Wright R3350 Twin Cyclone (4)
Engine rating	1200 hp	1200 hp	1700 hp	1600 hp	2200 hp

[*] First flight is for series prototype, data is for B-17G, B-24J, B-25J, B-26B, and B-29.

**North American Aviation
B-25H Mitchell**

Top left box: The Lockheed A-28 Hudson was essentially a military version of the Lockheed Super Electra, and served mainly with the RAF. *Top right box:* A Douglas A-20 Havoc attack bomber. *Immediately above:* A B-25B Mitchell. Compare these with the depictions on page 55, and then compare the B-25 and B-17 data in the table on page 56.

The grandest of all bombers to see service in World War II—and the only production aircraft ever to carry the USAAF's appellation 'very heavy bomber'—was the Boeing B-29 Superfortress. The idea for this super bomber evolved from the work done on the Experimental Bomber, Long Range project that had resulted in the B-15 in the late 1930s. A request for proposals went out to several planemakers early in 1940, calling for a bomber with range and payload double that of the B-17 or B-24. Because of their experience in the XB-15 and B-17 programs, Boeing had developed an expertise that helped it win the contract for the super bomber, which first flew on 21 September 1942, after being designated XB-29. It was flight tested during 1943 and rushed into production to make it available for service in April 1944.

USAAF chief General Hap Arnold was determined to keep the superfortresses together as a single unified force dedicated specifically to strategic bombing, rather than parceling them out to individual commands. He believed that by focusing all of the power of the whole B-29 forces on a specific objective, it could be used to fullest advantage. Arnold convinced the Joint Chiefs of Staff (of which he was a member) to create a single numbered Air Force—the Twentieth—to control the B-29s. This new Twentieth Air Force would be managed by the JCS themselves, bypassing the theater commander. The objective designated for the Twentieth would be the strategic bombardment of Japan, and Arnold himself felt that this effort had the potential of destroying Japan's will to continue the war without the need for a land invasion of Japan.

Under the auspices of the XX Bomber Command of the Twentieth Air Force commanded by General Curtis LeMay, the B-29s first went into combat on 5 June 1944, bombing Japanese forces in Bangkok from bases in India. Meanwhile, advanced bases had been established in China's Chengtu Valley from which the XX Bomber Command B-29s could reach Japan. The first raid against Japan itself took place on 14 July. Operations from the advanced bases

in China continued through the rest of the year, even as another B-29 force—the XXI Bomber Command—was setting up shop in the newly recaptured Marianas Islands in the Pacific.

Because of the long and treacherous supply lines required to keep the bases in China functioning, Arnold decided to concentrate the entire B-29 effort against Japan in the Marianas. Some XX Bomber Command B-29s, however, remained in India for a time to be used against targets in Southeast Asia. In January 1945, Arnold reassigned General LeMay to command the XXI Bomber Command in the final assault against Japan. In late February, disappointed with the results of high altitude precision bombing attacks on the assigned targets, LeMay decided to switch tactics. On 9 March he launched a ten day series of five maximum-effort low-level attacks against Japanese cities. Using incendiary bombs and more than twice as many aircraft than in any previous B-29 campaign, LeMay did more damage to Japan's war-making ability than in the previous three and a half years of the war. The first of the series of raids against Tokyo was, in fact, the most damaging raid of the war.

The raids were so massive that they nearly used up the entire XXI Bomber Command stock of incendiaries. This, combined with the diversion of the B-29s to support the Okinawa invasion, prevented another maximum effort until May 1945. By June, however, LeMay had an adequate supply line and a sufficient number of B-29s to make it possible to launch several 400-plane raids per week. By July, he was sending as many as 700 planes out on a single day.

On 16 July, the United States detonated the first atomic bomb and moved ahead with a plan to use these weapons in an effort to defeat Japan decisively before the invasion planned for November 1945. On 6 August, the B-29 Superfortress *Enola Gay* dropped an atomic bomb on the Japanese city of Hiroshima, and three days later another such weapon was dropped by a B-29 on Nagasaki. Within a week, Japanese leaders had agreed to accept the Allied demand for unconditional surrender.

Above: A flight of B-29 Superfortresses over China. *Below:* A 20th Bomber Command Superfortress overflies the famous Himalayan 'hump' en route to a target at Omura, Japan on 21 November 1944. The B-29 was bigger than any previous bomber, had a top speed of 360 mph, a ceiling of 31,850 feet and a ferry range of 5830 miles. The Soviets eventually stole the design from a B-29 forced down in the USSR, and made a direct copy—the Tu-4 Bull bomber, which evolved into their present-day Tu-20 Bear bomber.

Eddie Allen (*above*) had long been one of the nation's most respected pilot-consultants, and he was Boeing's best test pilot. He had test flown the B-15, B-17 and the Boeing Clipper; he knew more about the mechanical intricacies of these giants than any other man. In 1939, as the newly-appointed head of Boeing's Research Division, Eddie Allen directed planning and testing for the B-29. Allen took off in the second test prototype, the XB-29 (which had three-bladed propellers), on 18 February 1943. Twenty minutes later, he radioed Boeing Field that he was coming in with a wing on fire. The plane hit a packing plant, and the brilliant promise of Edmund T Allen was ended.

Boeing B-29 Superfortress

At left: The 40th Bomb Group B-29 Superfortress which was named for Eddie Allen. *Below:* A cutaway view of the same, showing the plane's rear bomb bay fully loaded. The planes were flown with both bomb bays loaded equally for balance. The long tube that passes over the bomb bays is the pressurized crawl space to the rear top gunner's position. Here also is seen the interior of the aircraft's wing, which could support approximately twice the gross weight for its surface area than any previous wing design (such as that of the B-17). Armament included .50 caliber machine guns—two each in three General Electric remote control turrets (bottom front and rear and top rear) and in the tail turret and two to four in the top forward turret; 20.000 pounds of bombs; and a 20 mm cannon which could be fitted to the tail turret in addition to that gunnery station's machine guns (of which an extra could be added in lieu of the cannon).

Below right: Each of the bombs stenciled on the fuselage of this B-29 signifies a mission completed.

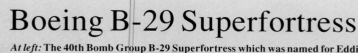

USAAF FIGHTERS OF WORLD WAR II

When the Japanese attacked Pearl Harbor on 7 December 1941, the first American fighters to engage them were Hawaii-based P-40 Warhawks. When the United States entered World War II, the Curtiss P-40 was the USAAF's front line fighter. The Warhawk was a fighter that already had been in service against the Japanese with the American Volunteer Group—the 'Flying Tigers'—in China. The P-40 was an outgrowth of the Model 75/P-36 series of radial-engined aircraft that Curtiss had produced in the 1930s.

In China, the American Volunteer Group (which evolved into the USAAF Fourteenth Air Force after the United States entered the war) ran up a very good record with the P-40 in air-to-air combat against the Japanese because of the tactics developed by its commander General Claire Chennault. Elsewhere the USAAF found the P-40 adequate but outclassed by the top Axis fighters. It

remained in front line service with the USAAF throughout 1942 and 1943, until more advanced aircraft arrived on the scene.

The Lockheed P-38 was conceived in 1937 as a high-speed air superiority fighter. It was intended to be twin-engined, yet light in weight to give it more range than other Air Corps fighters then in service. Having first flown on 27 January 1939, it went into production for both the United States and the British Royal Air Force. When the United States entered World War II, the P-38 was the fastest fighter available in service with the USAAF. This, combined with its long range capability, made it an invaluable asset during the fighting in the far-flung reaches of the South Pacific.

Its most famous mission came on 18 April 1943 when P-38s, based at Henderson Field on the hard-won island of Guadalcanal, intercepted and shot down a Japanese bomber carrying Admiral Isoroku Yamamoto, the mastermind

continued on page 68

The Curtiss P-36 Hawk, shown *at left* with its Pratt & Whitney radial engine, was the design base for the faster, farther-ranging Curtiss P-40 Warhawk, which is shown *below* with its Allison in-line engine. *At bottom, below:* A Lockheed P-38F Lightning at Gibraltar in 1942, prior to the invasion of North Africa. *At right:* A flight of P-38Ls.

Note: The US Army Air Corps (USAAC) became the US Army Air Forces (USAAF) on 20 June 1941. The USAAF in turn became the completely independent US Air Force (USAF) on 18 September 1947.

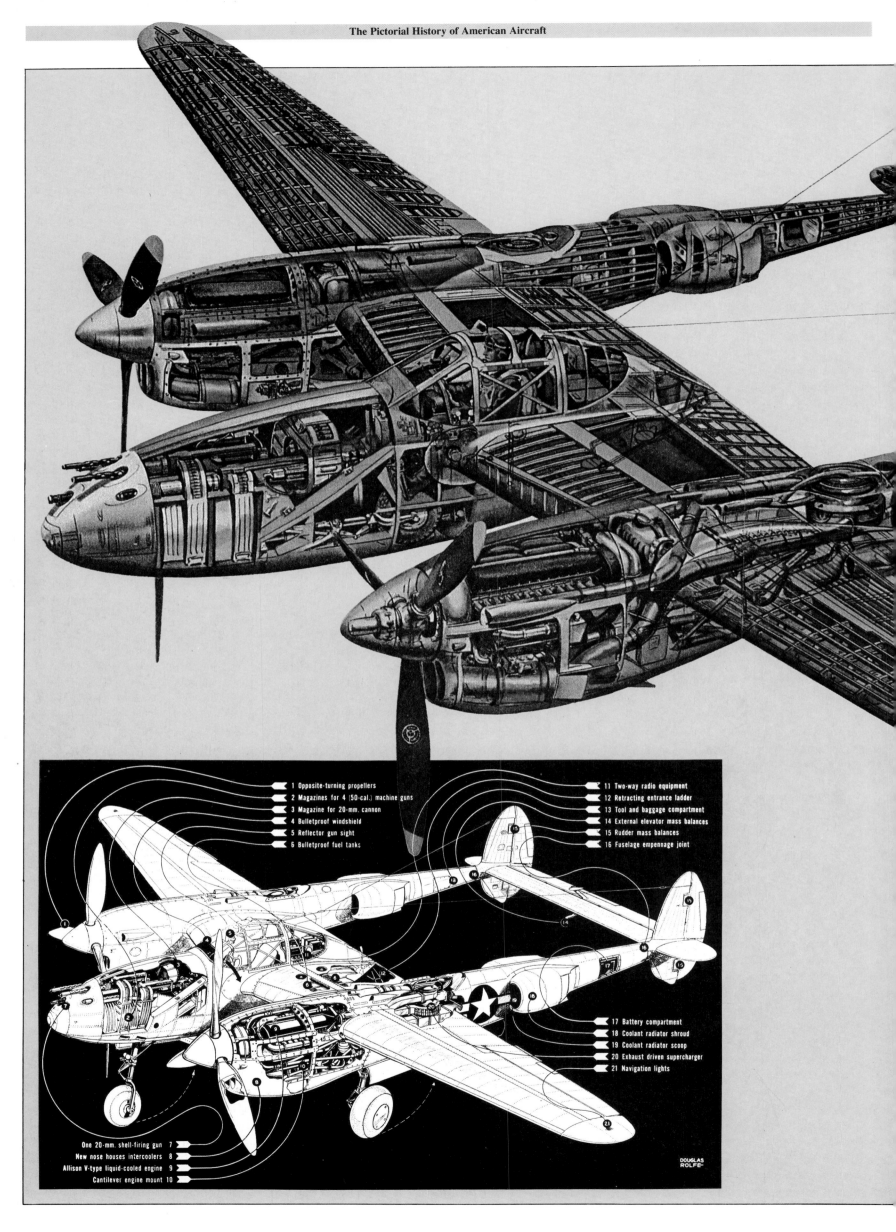

1 Opposite-turning propellers
2 Magazines for 4 (50-cal.) machine guns
3 Magazine for 20-mm. cannon
4 Bulletproof windshield
5 Reflector gun sight
6 Bulletproof fuel tanks

11 Two-way radio equipment
12 Retracting entrance ladder
13 Tool and baggage compartment
14 External elevator mass balances
15 Rudder mass balances
16 Fuselage empennage joint

17 Battery compartment
18 Coolant radiator shroud
19 Coolant radiator scoop
20 Exhaust driven supercharger
21 Navigation lights

One 20-mm. shell-firing gun 7
New nose houses intercoolers 8
Allison V-type liquid-cooled engine 9
Cantilever engine mount 10

DOUGLAS
ROLFE

52 ft

12 ft 10 in

37 ft 10 in

Lockheed P-38J Lightning

The 'Fork-Tailed Devil,' the potent Lockheed P-38 Lightning. *Clockwise from above:* Isometric views of the basic P-38 design; a P-38 pilot fires a burst of machine gun fire at speed; a sectional diagram showing the aircraft's various features; and a large, detailed 'ghost' view of a P-38J. The basic P-38 had a wing span of 52 feet, was 37 feet, 10 inches long, had a top speed in excess of 425 mph, and could attain an altitude of eight miles. The P-38's wing flaps were generally extended in combat situations, to tighten turns. Its twin-tailed look was born of practical considerations—the plane was to have powerful engines, lots of firepower and so on; by the time all that was asked of it was designed in, it had to have three fuselages!

continued from page 64
of Japan's fantastic successes in the early part of the war and the man who had planned the infamous attack on Pearl Harbor that brought the United States into World War II.

The P-38s were used throughout the world as air superiority fighters, bomber escorts and even as fighter bombers. Dick Bong, the highest scoring American ace of the war with 40 victories, flew the P-38, as did many others. Known to Germans as *Gabelschwanz Teufel* (fork-tailed devil), the P-38 racked up an impressive combat record and remained in production at Lockheed through the end of the war.

The heaviest single-engined fighter used by the USAAF in World War II was the Republic P-47 Thunderbolt, known to its crews as the 'Jug.' It was developed by aviation pioneer and Russian expatriate Alexander de Seversky in the late 1930s, with its first precursor being the Seversky XP-41 of 1939. Under new management, Seversky's firm became Republic Aviation, and the XP-41 became the YP-43. The design evolved first to P-44 and finally to XP-47A, neither of which were actually flight-tested but which did in turn evolve into the XP-47B, which first flew on 6 May 1941.

The first P-47Bs entered service with the USAAF shortly after Pearl Harbor, but because of technical problems affecting their deployment it was not until 15 April 1943 that a P-47 scored its first combat victory. This in itself is a good illustration of the importance of the P-38 and P-40. By the end of 1943, the P-47 was in service throughout the world—with the Fifth Air Force in the Pacific, with the Eighth and Ninth Air Forces in England, and with the Twelfth Air Force in the Mediterranean.

The early P-47s were of the 'razorback' cockpit variety, which offered the pilot little rear vision. In 1944, however, Republic began producing the P-47D with its 'bubble' canopy, affording its pilot a 360-degree field of view. This soon became the standard, and about three-quarters of the Thunderbolts built were of the P-47D variety.

Through the last two years of the war, the Jugs achieved an exceptional record, both as outstanding fighter-bombers and as air superiority fighters.

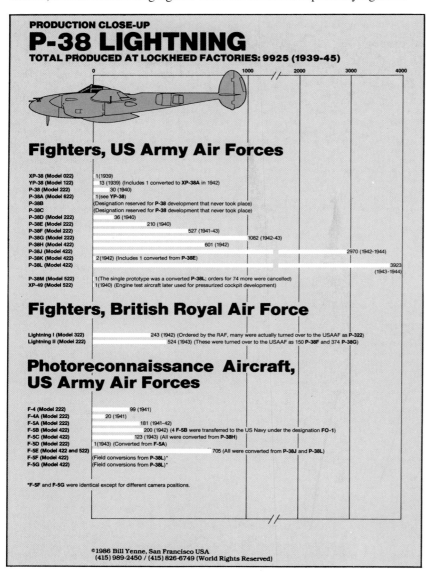

PRODUCTION CLOSE-UP

P-38 LIGHTNING
TOTAL PRODUCED AT LOCKHEED FACTORIES: 9925 (1939-45)

Fighters, US Army Air Forces

XP-38 (Model 022)	1(1939)
YP-38 (Model 122)	13 (1939) (Includes 1 converted to XP-38A in 1942)
P-38 (Model 222)	30 (1940)
P-38A (Model 622)	1(see YP-38)
P-38B	(Designation reserved for P-38 development that never took place)
P-38C	(Designation reserved for P-38 development that never took place)
P-38D (Model 222)	36 (1940)
P-38E (Model 222)	210 (1940)
P-38F (Model 222)	527 (1941-43)
P-38G (Model 222)	1082 (1942-43)
P-38H (Model 422)	601 (1942)
P-38J (Model 422)	2970 (1942-1944)
P-38K (Model 422)	2(1942) (Includes 1 converted from P-38E)
P-38L (Model 422)	3923 (1943-1944)
P-38M (Model 522)	1(The single prototype was a converted P-38L; orders for 74 more were cancelled)
XP-49 (Model 522)	1(1940) (Engine test aircraft later used for pressurized cockpit development)

Fighters, British Royal Air Force

Lightning I (Model 322)	243 (1942) (Ordered by the RAF, many were actually turned over to the USAAF as P-322)
Lightning II (Model 222)	524 (1943) (These were turned over to the USAAF as 150 P-38F and 374 P-38G)

Photoreconnaissance Aircraft, US Army Air Forces

F-4 (Model 222)	99 (1941)
F-4A (Model 222)	20 (1941)
F-5A (Model 222)	181 (1941-42)
F-5B (Model 422)	200 (1942) (4 F-5B were transferred to the US Navy under the designation FO-1)
F-5C (Model 422)	123 (1943) (All were converted from P-38H)
F-5D (Model 222)	1(1943) (Converted from F-5A)
F-5E (Model 422 and 522)	705 (All were converted from P-38J and P-38L)
F-5F (Model 422)	(Field conversions from P-38L)*
F-5G (Model 422)	(Field conversions from P-38L)*

*F-5F and F-5G were identical except for different camera positions.

©1986 Bill Yenne, San Francisco USA
(415) 989-2450 / (415) 826-6749 (World Rights Reserved)

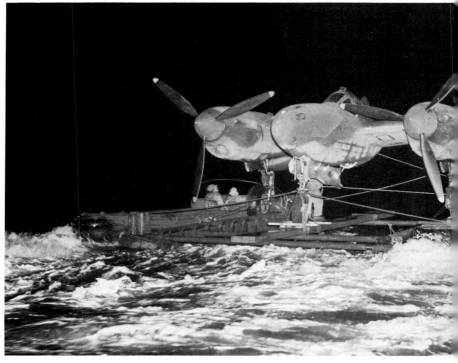

Above right: Lightnings in stack formation. The great US ace Dick Bong's P-38 bore the kill markings of 40 victories. *At right:* A P-38 being barged ashore in the Pacific Theater. *Far right:* A Curtiss P-40 of General Chennault's 14th Air Force in China. The distinctive tiger-face motif was a trademark of Chennault's 'Flying Tigers.' In the background is a Curtiss C-46 Commando, one of the USAAF's most important transport aircraft.

Above photos—Evolution of the 'Jug': The Republic P-43 of 1940 developed from the Seversky P-41 of 1939 *(top)*. *Center:* A 'Razorback' P-47B in prewar markings; and a bubble-canopy P-47D in France during the Ardennes offensive of 1944; camouflage no longer needed, the paint scheme returned to natural metal.

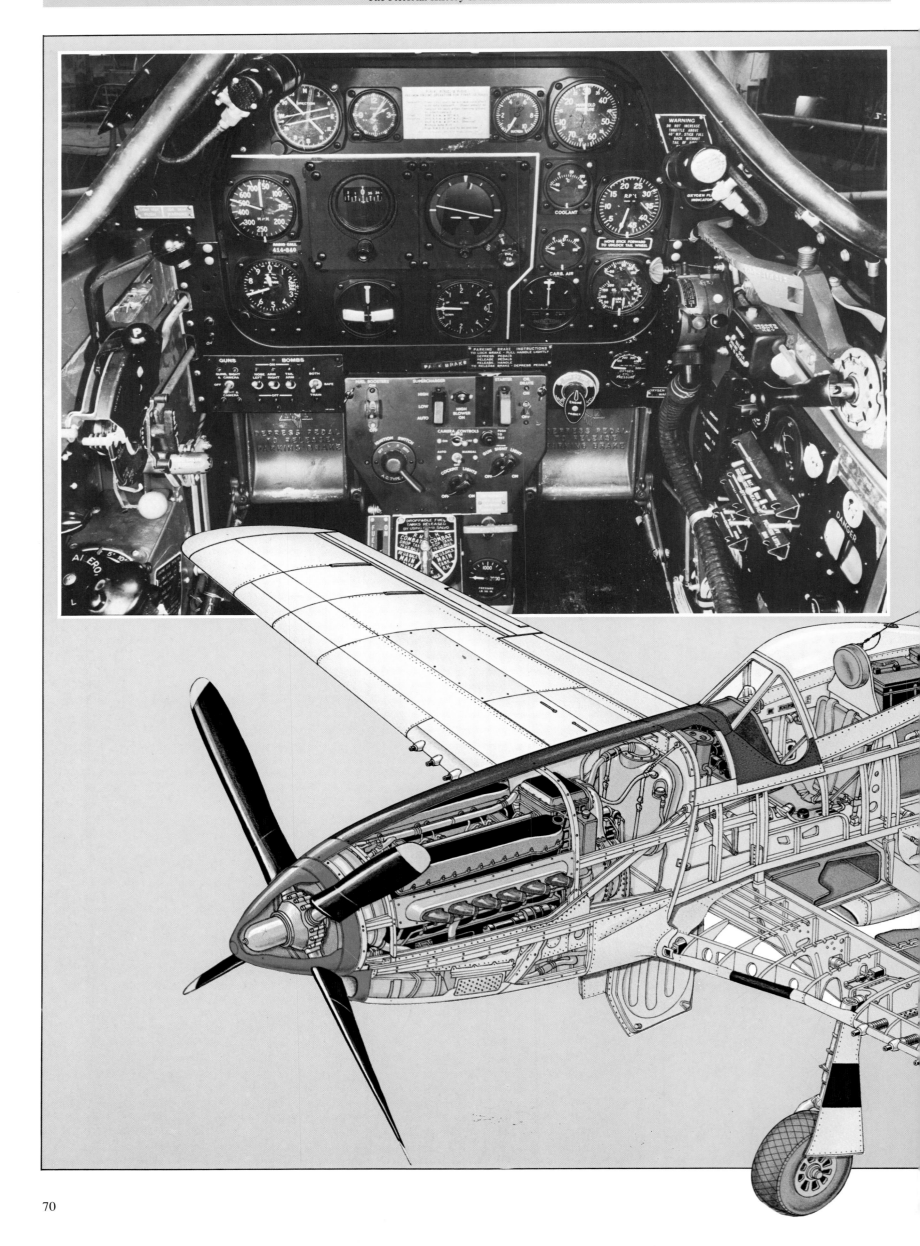

North American Aviation P-51D Mustang

Box at above left: Sitting in the pilot's seat of a P-51 Mustang. Most of the instrumentation is self-explanatory. Note that the artificial horizon (center of instrument panel) indicates some degree of slant—indicating that perhaps the plane seen here was parked at an angle for some reason. Note also that the speedometer goes up to 700 mph—perhaps to give a big allowance for diving speed. The top of the 'stick' can be seen at foreground left.

Box directly above: The neat, clean lines of the Mustang were born of production-simplification necessity. The greatest fighter plane of World War II outlived many of its fellow fighters in terms of numbers kept active after the war. The P-51's Cinderella tale is told on page 72 of this text. The speedometer markings notwithstanding, the P-51D had a top speed of 437 mph, and a service ceiling of 41,900 feet; with extra fuel tanks, it had a maximum range of 2300 miles. *At left* is a section view of some of the vital parts of a P-51D Mustang.

Of the great air superiority fighters of World War II, there is probably none other that has earned more votes for 'best' of its genre than the North American P-51 Mustang. Arriving relatively late in the war, it began its illustrious career after the great British Spitfires, German Bf-109s, American P-38s and Japanese Zeros had established their reputations. The P-51 the was long-awaited long-range fighter escort for the American strategic bombers penetrating the heart of the Reich, the first Allied fighter to pose a serious threat to Nazi interceptors in the skies over the fatherland itself. In the Pacific the Mustangs swarmed into Iwo Jima after its capture and used the former Japanese stronghold as a base from which to seize air superiority over the Japanese home islands.

Of World War II's great single piston-engine fighters, the P-51 was the only one to be conceived after the war began. Its origin is traceable to a British Air Ministry shopping trip to California in April 1940. The seven-month-old war had British aircraft factories working double time and still not meeting the RAF's demand for aircraft, so the Air Ministry was looking to buy additional types of American design which could be produced in the United States. The result was North American's Model 73, which was built in 117 days and which first flew in October 1940. The NA-73 bore a strong resemblance to the Curtiss Warhawk in the fuselage, although the wing and tail surfaces were distinctively its own. Its straight lines and sharp corners were dictated by the need for production simplicity. The first NA-73 crashed in November 1940 and it was not until a year later that the first NA-73 'Mustang I' arrived in England for service with the RAF. In the meantime, the Air Corps showed only a passing interest in the Mustang. Of the first ten that were built, the Air Corps purchased only two for its own flight tests and these were delivered to its Wright Field, Ohio flight test center under the designation XP-51 and the name 'Apache.'

When initially tested in England, the Mustang proved faster than the supermarine Spitfire V, but the RAF decided to retain the latter as its front-line interceptor because it would be easier to maintain a domestically-produced airplane for such a critical role. The RAF Mustangs were first assigned to the Royal Army Cooperation Command to serve in support of ground troops. An RAF Mustang had conducted a strafing attack on a Luftwaffe base in France on 10 May 1942, but they first saw action in large numbers and in their ground support role as part of the abortive British commando assault against Dieppe on the coast of Northern France.

Meanwhile, the first serious USAAF production order for the airplane destined to become the best USAAF fighter of World War II cast it as a dive bomber. Produced as North American's NA-97, it was basically an NA-73 fitted with dive brakes. Designated as A-36A and called Invader, 500 of the NA-73 dive bombers eventually were delivered to the USAAF with which they were to see service in campaigns in Sicily and Italy in 1943.

The A-36As were followed by the P-51A series which were intended for delivery to the USAAF and immediate transferral to the RAF as Mustang II. Most, however, were retained by the USAAF and assigned to the Fourteenth Air Force in the China-Burma-India theater, where they turned in a remarkably good performance against Japanese air and ground forces during 1943.

The Allison V-1710 engine was standard equipment in the 1000 RAF Mustangs and USAAF P-51s and 500 A-36As prior to the end of 1942. It had

Above: The Mustang as the A-36 Invader dive bomber (see text, this page). The quintessential Mustang, the P-51D *(at right)*, grew out of its earlier conception as the P-51B *(above right)*. Note the like fuselages, but the differences in canopies between the two.

made it a surprisingly reliable and capable airplane, but not a great airplane. Meanwhile, in the spring of 1942, the RAF experimented with the idea of retrofitting Mustangs with the Rolls Royce Merlin 61 engine. The resulting aircraft, called Mustang X, turned out to be amazingly powerful and the reviews of the Merlin-powered Mustang's performance were unanimous in their praise. Major Thomas Hitchcock, the American air attache in London, immediately recommended that his boss, USAAF commanding General Henry 'Hap' Arnold, consider acquiring Merlin-powered Mustangs for the USAAF. Coincidentally, the Merlin was being produced under license by Packard as the V-1650 in the United States, so North American was able to seriously plan a series of factory-built Merlin-powered Mustangs.

The major remaining problem with the Mustang was limited pilot visibility. A few Mustangs were retrofitted with the British Malcolm canopy that was used on the Supermarine Spitfire, but this measure was rejected as not going far enough. North American solved the problem with a full 'bubble' canopy which afforded the pilot a 360-degree field of vision. Developed as North American Model 106 (NA-106), the new Mustang went into full-scale production at Inglewood in February 1944 and at Dallas in July. The Dallas series was originally supposed to be designated as P-51E, but the P-51D designation was retained. It quickly became the definitive Mustang variant, with 7956 being built. Among these were 136 photo-reconnaissance aircraft that served as F-6D and 271 that went to the RAF as Mustang IV.

When it first arrived in the European theater in October 1943, the Packard-powered P-51B was still saddled with the stigma of being an attack plane in the A-36A mold. It was intended that the 354th Fighter Group—the first USAAF P-51B group—should be assigned to the Ninth Air Force, an England-based organization dedicated to tactical fighter-bomber operations. As luck would have it, however, the 354th was still under the control of the Eighth Air Force and the P-51Bs were pressed into service as long-range fighter escorts for the B-17 and B-24 heavy bombers that the Eighth was

At top, above: The P-51D's bubble canopy gave it a modern look, and let the pilot see much more. *Above:* The wooden wind tunnel model for the Mustang prototype. *At right:* Still flyin'—a Mustang in civvies (and a restored B-25) at the Chino Airport in the 1980s.

sending against strategic targets inside Germany. On 13 December 1943, the P-51Bs accompanied 649 heavy bombers to the U-boat pens at Kiel, bringing the first of many surprises to the homeland of the Nazi interceptors. Three days later a USAAF Mustang downed a German fighter for the first time, but only the first of many, for on 5 January 1944 Mustangs scored 18 victories. Just six days later Major James Howard shot down four Germans in a single engagement, earning himself the Congressional Medal of Honor.

Mustang production, particularly of the P-51D, moved at a rapid rate in 1944, and the fighter strength of the Eighth and Ninth Air Forces in England increased steadily. There were 14 P-51 fighter groups within the former and three within the latter. Of these, the 357th Fighter Group was the highest scoring group with 609 aerial victories. Meanwhile, there were four P-51 groups with the Fifteenth Air Force in Italy, four with the Fourteenth Air Force in China and three with the Fifth Air Force in the Pacific. The VII Fighter Command of the Seventh Air Force, which was organized to escort B-29 bombers on raids over Japan, also had three P-51 groups, designated as Very Long Range Fighter Groups, assigned. Based at airfields on the hard-won island of Iwo Jima, the P-51Ds of the VII Fighter Command began Very Long Range fighter operations on 16 April 1945, shooting down 34 Japanese interceptors in their first week over the Chrysanthemum Empire, and shooting up nearly 30 more on the ground during strafing runs.

The P-51 Mustang ended the war as the USAAF's top fighter—if not the top fighter of the war. Nearly half of the enemy aircraft shot down in Europe were claimed by Mustangs, while in the Pacific the P-51s controlled the skies of the Japanese homeland. From an inventory of 57 Mustangs at the end of 1942, USAAF inventory increased to 1165 at the end of 1943, 3914 at the end of 1944 and 5595 at the end of June 1945. After the war, Mustangs were retained in greater numbers than any other fighter type, with 3303 still remaining in service at the end of 1946, though most were being transferred to units of the Air National Guard. In 1947, as the USAAF became the US Air Force, the P-51 was redesignated as F-51.

The largest of the principal USAAF fighters was the Northrop P-61 Black Widow. Designed as a night flyer, the huge twin-engined plane was in the same size and weight class as a medium *bomber*.

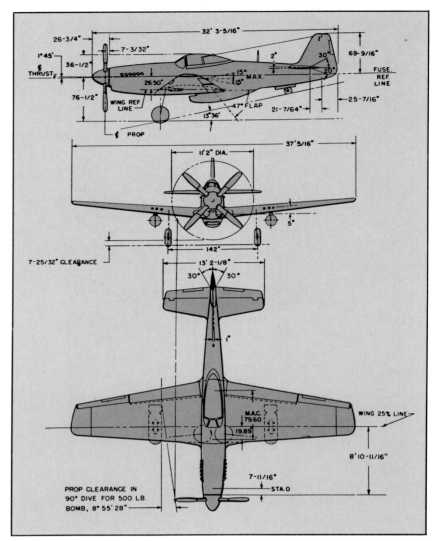

USAAF Fighters of World War II

Specifications[*]	Lockheed P-38 Lightning	Curtiss P-40 Warhawk	Republic P-47 Thunderbolt	North American P-51 Mustang	Northrop P-61 Black Widow
First Flight[*]	1939	1938	1941	1940	1942
Wing span	52'	37'4"	40'9"	37'	66'
Length	37'10"	33'4"	36'4"	32'3"	49'7"
Gross weight	17,500 lb	8500 lb	13,275 lb	10,100 lb	29,700 lb
Cruising speed	350 mph	290 mph	350 mph	413 mph	300 mph
Range	2600 mi	700 mi	800 mi	950 mi	1200 mi
Engine	Allison V-1710 (2)	Packard V-1650	Pratt & Whitney R-2800	Packard V-1650	Pratt & Whitney R-2800 (2)
Engine rating	1425 hp	1300 hp	2800 hp	1720 hp	2000 hp

[*] First flight for series prototypes, data for P-38J, P-40F, P-47N, P-51D and P-61B.

Below left: A Mustang with wing tanks warms up for takeoff in the 1940s. *At left:* Dimensional views of the P-51D, some examples of which were redesignated F-51 (see text). *Below and overleaf:* The Northrop P-61 Black Widow was the first USAAF fighter to be specifically designed as a night fighter; from experience gained by the Allies as World War II progressed, it was seen that the ideal night fighter would feature heavy armament and armor, reliability, advanced radar and the solidity required of a heavy gun platform. The first P-61s carried single remote control turrets, but the turrets proved unreliable, and most already-produced P-61s had their turrets removed. Armed with four .50 caliber machine guns and four 20 mm cannons, the P-61 proved a deadly opponent for any Axis airplane in the nighttime skies. First operational in July of 1944, the Black Widow became the standard US night fighter by the end of the War. The last version of the Black Widow was the F-15A Reporter reconnaissance plane, which served until 1952.

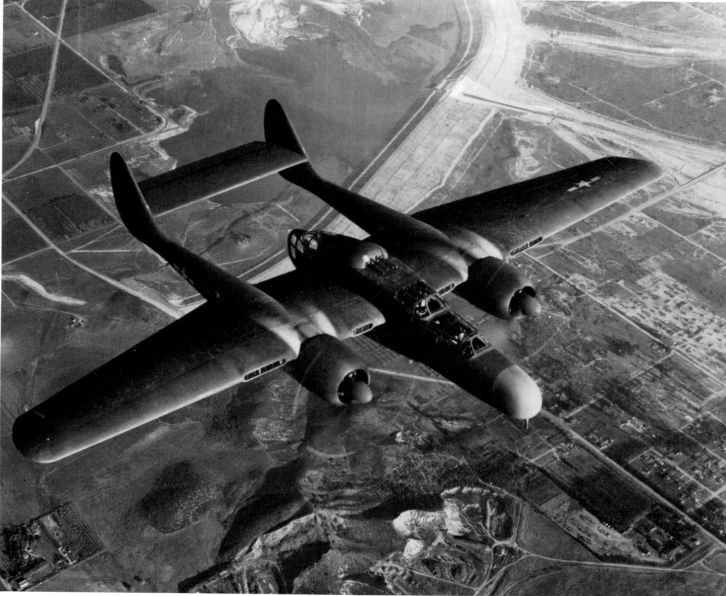

USAAF noncombat aircraft of World War II: *Above:* The Stearman PT-13 Kaydett was an important basic trainer. *At left:* The cockpit of the AT-6 Texan *(below)*—the Air Training Command's most-used trainer. The most-used transport of the Air Transport Command was the C-47 *(below right)*. The C-53 *(at right)* was essentially a C-47 tailored for paratroops.

These pages: One of the world's best known general aviation aircraft, the Piper J-3 Cub. Back in 1929, the Taylor Brothers Aircraft Corporation moved from Rochester, New York to Bradford, Pennsylvania in search of new investors. William T Piper, Sr, and Ralph Lloyd, partners in a Bradford oil company, invested $800 each in the Taylor company—headed by Gilbert Taylor, a self-taught aeronautical engineer. With his late brother, Gordon, Taylor had developed a 90 hp monoplane with a two seat, side-by-side design, billed as the Taylor Chummy, which was never popular. At William Piper's suggestion, Taylor went to a lighter, simpler design which was named the E-2; a good design, but terribly underpowered.

The Taylor Brothers Aircraft Corporation went bankrupt in 1931, and William Piper snapped it up for less than $1000; he retained Taylor as chief engineer of the company. Piper tried a more powerful engine, the newly developed Continental A-40, in the E-2, and the E-2 Cub was finally certified by the Bureau of Air Commerce in 1931; 24 E-2s were sold in 1932 at $1325 apiece. Gilbert Taylor went off to Ohio, where he founded the successful Taylor Young Airplane Company, producing upgraded versions of his early side-by-side designs. In 1936, Piper upgraded the E-2 and called it the Piper J-2 Cub. Shortly after this, the Bradford plant burned down, and Piper operations moved to Lock Haven, Pennsylvania, to become the Piper Aircraft Corporation.

The J-3 Cub was born in 1938, with a newly-redesigned vertical stabilizer. Only a few of these were sold in the 40 hp design when Continental, Lycoming and Franklin brought out competitive 50 hp engines, all of which were available in the J-3. The 50 horsepower J-3 Cubs were the first to use the famous 'Cub yellow' paint scheme, which was standard even when the last J-3 was built in 1947. In 1940, the J-3 Cub was certified with both the Continental and the Lycoming 65 horsepower engine. Soon, the Civilian Pilot Training Program (instituted on the eve of World War II) created a special demand for J-3s, bringing Piper's production up to 3000 Cubs per year. By the end of the Program (by then known as the War Training Service) in 1944, J-3 Cubs had helped to train some 430,000 primary flight students. Also during World War II, the US Army procured 5671 Cubs, which were designated 0-59s and L-4s. All in all, some 14,125 J-3s were built by the end of production.

US NAVY AIRCRAFT OF WORLD WAR II

During World War II the US Navy operated as wide a variety of aircraft as any other air service in history. Most notable of these were, of course, the planes that were peculiar to the needs of a naval air arm, such as seaplanes and carrier-based aircraft. The former included everything from huge transports to tiny observation planes carried on catapults at the aft end of cruisers and battleships. The most widespread use of seaplanes was as patrol bombers, and the most widely used US Navy patrol bomber was the Consolidated PBY Catalina. The PBY was, in fact, the most widely used flying boat in history. Consolidated's experience with such aircraft dated back to the XPY of 1929 and the XP2Y of 1932. These twin-tailed Navy patrol bombers were identical in size (100 foot span by 61-foot, 9-inch length) and bore a passing resemblance to the later XP34 (104 foot span by 63-foot, 6-inch length), which first flew in 1935 and which was the true prototype PBY. With its designation changed from PCY (Patrol, Consolidated, third) to PBY (Patrol Bomber, Consolidated, first) the Catalina was ordered into production in 1936 with a span of 104 feet and a length of 65 feet, 2 inches.

When World War II began in Europe, Australia, Britain, Canada and France joined the US Navy in ordering Catalinas. On 26 May 1941, a British Catalina was responsible for locating the infamous German battleship *Bismarck*, prior to the great North Atlantic naval battle in which that warship was sunk by His Majesty's Navy.

The US Navy's Catalinas entered the war in service at coastal air stations throughout the United States, as well as in Hawaii and the Philippines. However, most of the PBYs in Hawaii were destroyed in the Pearl Harbor attack on 7 December 1941. Revenge was sweet, however, as a Hawaii-based PBY was responsible for sighting the Japanese fleet prior to the decisive Battle of Midway in 1942.

The versatile patrol bomber then went on to an extensive career, playing a role in every major action involving the US Navy. Catalinas also continued to serve with the RAF Coastal Command, other British Empire air forces, and even the USAAF, which purchased them for air-sea rescue under the designation OA-10. In addition to those PBYs built by Consolidated, a handful of Catalinas were built by the Naval Aircraft factory as PBN and by Boeing Canada as PB2B.

Other important World War II flying boats included the four-engined Consolidated PB2Y Coronado (1937), the Martin PBM Mariner (1940) and

Above: A PBY Catalina at Watton-Griston airfield in England. *Above, at top:* A flight of Grumman J2F Ducks. *Above right:* A Consolidated PB2Y Coronado in air transport configuration. *Below:* A Consolidated PBY Catalina in RAF markings, one of which was responsible for hunting down the notorious German battleship *Bismarck*. *Facing page, below:* SBD Dauntless divebombers provided the US Navy with fearsome airpower in

World War II. Here Dauntless SBDs overfly the carrier USS *Enterprise* somewhere in the Pacific. *Facing page, above:* Douglas TBD Devastator torpedo bombers performed well enough up until 60 percent of them were lost at the Battle of Midway; see text, page 88.

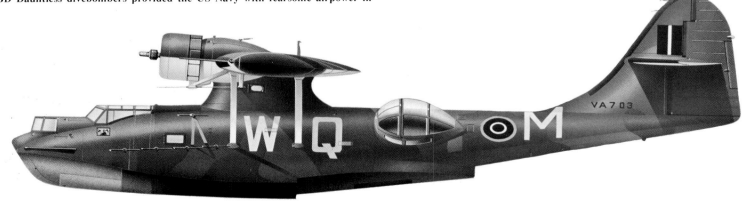

the enormous Martin PB2M Mars (1942), an airplane so huge that it was allegedly configured with separate mess halls for officers and enlisted men.

For aircraft carrier operations, the US Navy had developed specialized types of squadrons—fighting (VF), scout bombing (VSB) and torpedo bombing (VTB)—each with its own specialized types of aircraft. Among the scout bombers, the Douglas SBD (Scout Bomber, Douglas) Dauntless was nothing short of legendary. It evolved out of a series of monoplane attack bombers developed by Northrop in the late 1930s and it became a Douglas project when Northrop merged into Douglas in 1938. The first SBD flew on 1 May 1940 and it was in service aboard the Navy's carriers by the time the United States entered World War II. The first enemy ship sunk by the US Navy in the war—a Japanese submarine—fell to the dive bombing attack of an SBD from the carrier USS *Enterprise* just three days after Pearl Harbor. From there the 'diving Dauntless' went on to play a major role in the war in the Pacific through 1944. During that time, SBDs sank numerous enemy vessels, among them a battleship, six aircraft carriers and eleven other major warships.

The successor to the Dauntless, and itself a legend of sorts, was the Curtiss SB2C Helldiver. Though the prototype first flew in 1940, the program was so plagued by technical difficulties that in April 1943 a congressional investigation revealed it to be 'hopelessly behind schedule.' In fact, it was not until November 1943 that the Helldiver was ready for combat. From then on, however, the SB2C readily proved itself to be a worthy successor to the SBD.

Above: An early Martin PBM in prewar high visibility colors. *Below:* A flight of legendary Dauntless SBD-3s flies over coastal lands in the early 1940s. *Above right:* The last combat biplane produced in the US, the Curtiss SBC Helldiver, is here illustrated in contrast to its later namesake (the last bearer of the Helldiver appellation), the Curtiss SB2C Helldiver,

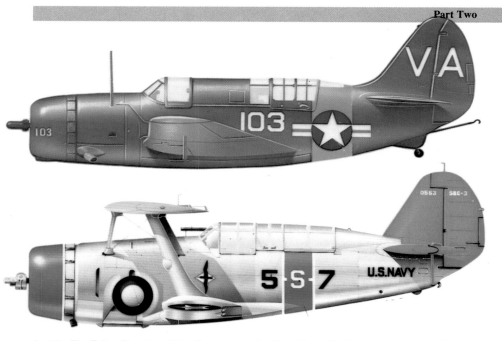

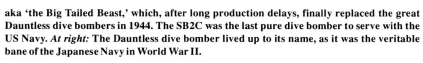

aka 'the Big Tailed Beast,' which, after long production delays, finally replaced the great Dauntless dive bombers in 1944. The SB2C was the last pure dive bomber to serve with the US Navy. *At right:* The Dauntless dive bomber lived up to its name, as it was the veritable bane of the Japanese Navy in World War II.

In the area of torpedo bombers, the Navy entered the war with the Douglas TBD (a first cousin of the Dauntless) as its principal player. It performed reasonably well in the Battle of the Coral Sea in May 1942 helping, despite heavy losses, to sink the Japanese carrier *Shoho*. At the Battle of Midway in June 1942, however, 60 percent of the Navy's prewar stock of TBDs were shot down in the space of a few hours. The US Navy won the battle but they clearly needed a faster torpedo bomber.

The answer lay in the big Grumman TBF Avenger, which first flew in August 1941. So critical was the need for the Avenger that General Motors was asked to join Grumman in the production pool. Between January 1942 and December 1943, Grumman produced 2290 Avengers, while between November 1942 and September 1945 General Motors produced 7543 under the designation TBM. After 1943, Avengers were assigned to every American carrier and committed to every major naval action in the Pacific, including the successful all-air power assaults on the two largest battleships ever built, the *Yamato* and the *Musashi*.

At left: This Grumman TBF Avenger was the sole survivor of the first attack against the Japanese carriers at the Battle of Midway. *Above and right:* A formation of Avengers over the Pacific, and an early TBF-1 Avenger in camouflage colors. *Below:* SM2C Helldivers return from a strike.

Following the war, Avengers remained with the United States fleet until 1954, but were retained until much later with various allied navies.

The name Grumman has always gone hand in hand with American naval aviation, and nowhere is this more true than with the Grumman 'carrier cat' fighters of World War II. Grumman had three biplane carrier fighters of some note under its belt in 1936 when it began work on its F4F project, an all-metal monoplane with the established Grumman trademark of a main landing gear that folded *into the side* of the fuselage below the wings.

The first F4F, flown in 1937, lost out to the Brewster Buffalo in its first try for a Navy contract the following year. However, in 1940 an improved F4F-3 was offered to, and accepted by, the Navy. Before the end of the year it was in service with the British Royal Air Force under the name Martlet, and with the US Navy under the name Wildcat. The F4F-4, introduced in 1941, had folding wings for aircraft carrier storage, a feature common to subsequent types. When the United States entered World War II, the Wildcat was the Navy's leading fighter, a role that it would retain until edged out by its brother, the Hellcat. Grumman built 1977 Wildcats itself and General Motors built another 5927 under the FM desgination. The Wildcat's overall war record was impressive. In aerial combat, Navy and Marine Corps pilots (including Major Joe Foss with 26 victories) shot down 1327 enemy aircraft against a loss of only 191 Wildcats.

The Grumman F6F Hellcat, the F4F's worthy successor, was first flown in June 1942. It did not go into large scale production until the end of the year, but in 1943 it was streaming out the factory doors at a rate of almost 50 a week! It entered service quickly and soon equipped every fighter squadron on every major aircraft carrier in the Pacific, where it developed an outstanding reputation in air-to-air combat against Japanese aircraft in such battles as the extraordinary Marianas Turkey Shoot of June 1944. In fact, over half of the Japanese planes shot down by Navy fighters during the war were claimed by Hellcats, whose kill ratio in combat was a spectacular 19 to 1. After the war, Hellcats continued in service with both the US Navy and the British Royal Navy until the end of the decade, and with the French navy in Indochina into the 1950s.

A gull-winged masterpiece, the Vought F4U Corsair was one of the best naval fighters in World War II. She was the fourth in a line of US Navy fighters to come from the firm founded by Chance Milton Vought in 1917. This line began with 20 float-equipped biplane FU-1s that served aboard Navy battleships in 1927 and 1928. Officially named Corsair by the Navy, it was only one of several planes to which Vought had given that name.

The Corsair's first carrier trials, which took place in September 1942, were not entirely satisfactory, so the first operational deployment was not aboard a carrier at sea, but rather to land-based Marine units on Guadalcanal on 12 February 1943. Navy fighter units began using Corsairs operational in the Pacific in September, however, and by the end of the war there were 19 Fleet Air Arm squadrons equipped with them. In April 1944, the British Royal Navy began receiving Corsairs and soon after deliveries began to New Zealand.

While the Corsair served throughout the world during the war, it achieved most of its notoriety in the Pacific theater where it quickly established its superiority over the Japanese Mitsubishi A6M Zero. The Zero was an extremely maneuverable fighter that had outperformed every Allied fighter in the Pacific throughout 1942. Navy and Marine Corps pilots established an 11.3 to 1 kill ratio over the Japanese, shooting down 2140 enemy aircraft for the loss of 189 Corsairs in aerial combat.

The top three Corsair aces also won the Congressional Medal of Honor for their heroic flying. They were Major Greg 'Pappy' Boyington (28 victories), Lt Robert Hanson (25 victories) and Major Kenneth Walsh (21 victories). British Corsair pilot Lt RA Gray won the Victoria Cross—his nation's highest decoration—posthumously for a successful attack on Japanese ships during a strike on Shiogama.

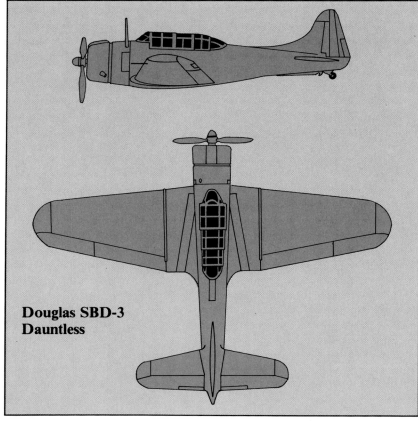

**Douglas SBD-3
Dauntless**

At left: **An F4F-4 Wildcat with large center dots in its star insignia; these dots were later painted out to avoid confusion with the Japanese 'Rising Sun.'** *At top, above:* **A Vought F4U Corsair, the US Navy and US Marine Corps' great World War II fighter.**

Grumman TBF (General Motors TBM-3) Avenger in 1943 markings.

Grumman F4F Wildcat in pre-1942 markings.

Grumman F6F Hellcat with the insignia that was employed between 29 June and 14 August 1943.

Vought F4U Corsair in post-1947 markings.

US Navy Carrier Aircraft of World War II					
*Specifications**	**Grumman F4F Wildcat**	**Douglas SBD Dauntless**	**Grumman TBF Avenger****	**Vought F4U Corsair**	**Grumman F6F Hellcat**
Type	Fighter	Dive Bomber	Torpedo Bomber	Fighter	Fighter
*First Flight**	1937	1940	1941	1940	1942
Wing span	38'0"	41'6"	54'2"	41'	42'10"
Length	28'9"	33'	40'	33'4"	33'7"
Gross weight	7002 lb	9353 lb	13,667 lb	12,039 lb	12,441 lb
Cruising speed	330 mph	252 mph	145 mph	359 mph	375 mph
Range	1690 mi	1115 mi	1215 mi	1015 mi	1590 mi
Engine	Pratt & Whitney R1830	Wright R1820	Wright R2600	Pratt & Whitney R2800	Pratt & Whitney R2800
Engine rating	1000 hp	1000 hp	1700 hp	2000 hp	1600 hp

* First flight is for series prototype, data is for F4F-3, SBD-5, TBF-1, F4U-1, and F6F-3.
** Although designed originally by Grumman, most Avengers were manufactured by General Motors as TBM.

Equally important to its aerial combat record was the Corsair's versatility. It was superb as a close-support aircraft and was a welcome sight overhead for American forces as they island-hopped their way toward Japan. During the brutal battle for Okinawa during April 1945 the plane was nicknamed 'Whistling Death' by the Japanese and for the same reason the Americans called her the 'Angel of Okinawa.'

During the invasion of Eniwetok, three Corsairs were in action for nine hours and 40 minutes. This is believed to be the longest sustained combat flight by a single-place aircraft.

Total wartime production of the Corsair reached 12,126. Most of these were produced by Vought, with Goodyear building 4017 and Brewster 735. After May 1948 production started to include additional F4U-5N night fighters and F4U-5P photo-reconnaissance aircraft as Vought moved its factory location from Hartford, Connecticut to Dallas, Texas, where F4U-5Ns were built through September 1951.

On 3 July 1950, a week after the Korean War began, F4U-4Bs from the USS *Valley Forge* (CV-45) went into action. Once again the Corsair was in combat, and although jets were now fully operational in the Navy and Marine Corps, the Corsair proved ideal for ground support and night fighter duties. One Navy F4U-5N pilot, Lt Guy Bordelon, for example, became an ace in just 18 days.

The first Corsair pilot to shoot down a MiG-15 over Korea was Marine Captain Jesse Folmar. When he and his wingman were jumped by four MiGs, Folmar was able to turn inside one and blast him. Shortly thereafter, Folmar himself was shot down by another MiG. He bailed out, however, and was rescued.

The outbreak of the Korean War led to additional orders for 214 F4U-5Ns and for a 101 special winterized F4U-5NL. Orders for an armored Corsair optimized for ground attack were also forthcoming. Originally designated as F4U-6, this version was delivered under the 'attack' designation AU-1. The AU was armed with four 20mm cannons like the F4U-5 but also carried a choice of ten rockets or two tons of bombs. Armor plate was added beneath the cockpit and around the fuel tank and engine. Vought delivered 111 AU-1s between December 1951 and October 1952.

The final Corsair variant was the F4U-7, of which 94 were built for the French Navy in 1952. The F4U-7 was powered by the R-2800-18W engine and thus was similar to the F4U-4B in American service. The French Corsairs flew attack missions from the carrier *Lafayette* off Indochina through 1954 and aboard the *Arromanches* in the Mediterranean during the 1956 Suez crisis.

The Corsair served with the US Navy until 1955, longer than any other World War II-era aircraft. The French Navy retained their Corsairs until 1964.

Today, Corsairs of various types are still flown on the air race circuit. Some of these include the survivors of a batch of 10 to 18 F2Gs that were built by Goodyear at the end of World War II with 3000 hp Wasp major engines. Another is the Budweiser Lite-sponsored Corsair that made its debut at the 1982 Reno Air Races. Powered by a 4000 hp Pratt & Whitney R-4360, it is an F4U-1 that was specially modified by Steve Hinton and Jim Maloney. In the process of stripping the layers of paint from the Corsair, they discovered seven small Japanese flags, indicating that this anonymous F4U-1 had been flown by an American ace some 40 years before.

Below and above right: Designed for maximum performance by the simple expedient of building the smallest possible airplane around the largest possible engine, the Vought F4U Corsair had a kill ratio of 11:1 against Japanese fighter planes. Its top speed of 470 mph and service ceiling of 41,400 feet were just some of this great fighter plane's outstanding characteristics. Of all fighters in production during World War II, the Corsair continued in production the longest, its manufacture finally being halted in 1952 after some 12,571 aircraft had been built. The French Navy used Corsairs long after World War II—until 1965, and in the Korean War, American Corsairs were deadly night fighters and ground-support craft, and at least one bagged a MiG-15 jet in a dogfight! Designed in 1938, the Corsair established itself as one of the most formidable fighters of dangerous fighter-heavy World War II. Hated by the enemy and celebrated by the Allies, the Corsair was an ultra-effective combat airplane. Corsairs flew some 64,051 sorties from 1943 through the end of World War II.

Part Three

The Postwar Years

POSTWAR NAVAL AIRCRAFT

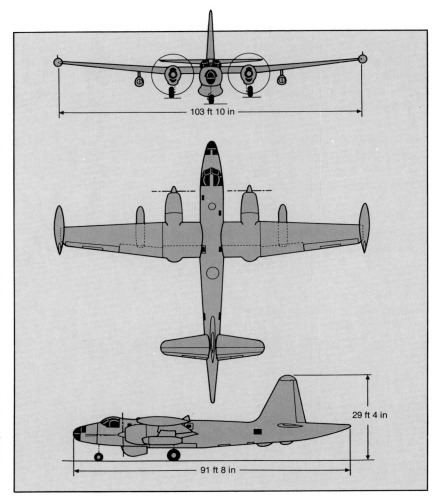

he US Air Force emerged from World War II dedicated to the mission of developing intercontinental strategic bombers for the purpose of maintaining peace through nuclear deterrence. For the first time since the founding of the United States, the Navy found that *it* was no longer the first line of defense against foreign aggression. Furthermore, after the establishment of the US Air Force in 1947, the new Department of Defense decided to concentrate all of its air transport assets with the Military Air Transport Service, which was set up *under* the Air Force in 1948.

Having lost not only its traditional role but the transport aircraft as well, the Navy focused its direction in the development of noncarrier-based aircraft on very long range patrol airplanes. The mission was antisubmarine warfare, but the underlying fact was that the Navy, as well as the Air Force, had the ability to fly intercontinental bombing missions with nuclear weapons.

The first postwar Navy patrol plane was the Lockheed P2V Neptune, which first flew on 17 May 1945 and entered service the following year. A twin-engined aircraft, it had a range that exceeded that of many four-engined bombers of the war era. In fact, one P2V, the *Truculent Turtle*, flew nonstop from Australia to Ohio on 29 September 1946, setting a nonrefueled distance record of 11,236 miles, a record which stood for a dozen years. The Neptune was an extraordinarily durable and successful airplane, serving not only with the US Navy but with Britain, France, the Netherlands and Japan, to name a few. It remained in production at Lockheed until 1962 and in service with the US Navy until 1970. The P2V (redesignated as P-2 in 1962) was also extremely versatile. In one test, a fully loaded Neptune took off from the deck of the aircraft carrier USS *Coral Sea* and flew a 4000 mile mission.

During and before World War II, flying boats had been an integral part of the Naval air arm. In the immediate postwar years, Consolidated Catalinas and Martin Mariners were retained—principally as rescue aircraft—but only one new major type was developed. This aircraft, the Martin PSM Marlin, was first flown in 1948 and 227 were delivered to the Navy as patrol bombers between 1951 and 1960. When the last Marlin was retired in November 1967, the Navy ended 56 years of flying boat operations.

Above: **Three views of the Lockheed P2V-7 Neptune.** *Below:* **The P2V Neptune** *Truculent Turtle,* **which set an unrefueled flying record nonstop from Australia to Ohio in 1946.** *At right:* **The Neptune P2V-4 patrol plane. Note belly radome and fixed wingtip tanks.**

In the meantime, the Navy had the only jet-powered flying boat—the Martin P6M Seamaster, which first flew in 1955. Only 11 Seamasters had been built when the Navy suddenly terminated the program in 1959. The Seamaster had the distinction of being the last airplane type ever built by the company started half a century earlier by Glenn Martin.

The most successful postwar Naval patrol bomber is the Lockheed P-3 Orion (P3V before 1962), which is the successor to the Lockheed Neptune. First flown in 1959, the Orion entered service in 1962. Still in production in the late 1980s, the P-3 is in service not only with the US Navy but also with the naval air arms of Australia, Japan, the Netherlands, New Zealand, Norway and Canada (where it is known as the CP-140 Aurora). For its antisubmarine role, the Orion is equipped with magnetic anomaly detectors, radar, passive and active sonobouys, torpedoes, depth charges and (since 1977) Harpoon antiship missiles.

Below: The most advanced flying boat ever built, the Martin P6M Seamaster. *Above:* A US Navy Lockheed P-3 Orion anti-submarine warfare (ASW) plane rides shotgun over the US Navy submarine SS *Chopper. Above right:* The Orion as a meteorological test bed, dispensing silver iodide into the clouds to precipitate a rain storm. *Opposite:* A Navy P-3C Orion in a low flight over California coastal waters. *Opposite, below:* The Grumman S-2 Tracker was the first carrier-based (and carrier catapult-launched) ASW aircraft.

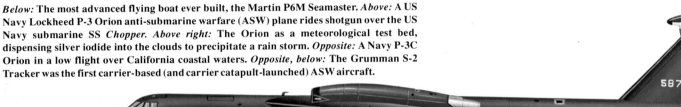

US Navy Postwar Patrol Aircraft

Specifications[*]	Lockheed P2V(P-2) Neptune	Martin P5M Marlin	Grumman S-2(S2F) Tracker	Martin P6M Seamaster	Lockheed P-3(P3V) Orion
First Flight[*]	1945	1948	1952	1955	1959
Wing span	101'4"	102'7"	72'7"	99'8"	118'2"
Length	91'8"	100'2"	43'6"	134'4"	116'10"
Gross weight	67,500 lb	76,595 lb	29,150 lb	167,011 lb	135,000 lb
Cruising speed	188 mph	159 mph	150 mph	540 mph	235 mph
Range	4293 mi	2471 mi	968 mi	1595 mi	5200 mi
Engine	Wright R3350 Cyclones (2) Wright J34 Turbojets (2)	Wright R3350 Cyclones (2)	Wright R1820 (2)	Allison J71 Turbojets (4)	Allison T56 Turboprops (4)
Engine rating	2400 hp	3420 hp	1525 hp	9500 lb	4900 hp

[*] First flights are for series prototypes, data is for P2V-7, P5M-2, S-2A, YP6M-1 and P-3C

All of the US Navy's carrier-based aircraft since the Second World War fit roughly the same mission categories that they did during the war, except that scout bomber and torpedo bomber squadrons were merged into a single attack bomber classification. Of these, the AD series Skyraider was among the most important. First flown on 18 March 1945 under the designation SBT2D-1, the Skyraider entered service in November 1946 with the AD designation. Capable of carrying a very large bomb load, the Skyraider was a mainstay of the Navy's carrier-based offensive efforts during the Korean War. More than a decade later, the AD (A-1 after 1962) found itself at war again, this time in Vietnam. A-1 Skyraiders served not only with the US Navy in Southeast Asia, but with the US Air Force and the South Vietnamese air force as well. It was at the hands of Navy pilots that the venerable Skyraider achieved a distinction that is extremely rare for attack bombers: shooting down two North Vietnamese MiG-17 jet fighters!

Above: **The 'hunter' part of a Skyraider hunter/killer team, an A-1E (formerly AD-5) returns to its carrier, the USS** *Constellation***, after a combat mission over Vietnam in 1967.** *At top:* **Fully-loaded Skyraiders of Attack Squadron 52 in a breaking flight formation.**

Below: Hunter-killer team: An AD-5 Skyraider, with its long two place side-by-side cockpit (all the space in back is packed with electronic surveillance and countermeasures equipment) and underbelly radome, accompanies and acts as bird dog for the heavily-armed AD-6 single-seater Skyraider just behind it. This was a familiar duo in the Vietnam conflict, and Navy pilots flying A-1Hs (formerly AD-6s) even bagged two MiGs! The South Vietnamese Air Force also flew Skyraiders. *At right, left and right:* Views of the definitive 'Able Dogs', the AD-6 (A-1H after 1962), and AD-5 (A-1E after 1962) Skyraiders.

Douglas AD-6

Douglas AD-5

Another important postwar attack bomber, which was also built by Douglas, was the tiny A-4 (A4D before 1962) Skyhawk. Designed by ace designer Ed Heinemann, the small, fast bomber was nicknamed 'Heinemann's hot rod.' First flown in 1954, the Skyhawk continued in production until 1979 and in service well into the late 1980s. During its career the Skyhawk served with the US Navy in Vietnam, with the Israeli air force in the 1973 Mideast War and with the Argentine navy during the 1982 war with Britain over the Falkland Islands (Argentine designation: Las Ilas Malvinas).

The successor to the A-4 Skyhawk was the all-weather Grumman A-6 Intruder, which was first flown in 1960 and continues to serve the US Fleet as an electronic warfare aircraft, as well as an attack bomber.

At top, above: **Flying A-4s, the US Navy's Blue Angels engage in aerobatics near San Francisco's Golden Gate Bridge in October of 1983.** *At top, right:* **A 'boxed,' suitable-for-framing portrait of the Blue Angels putting their Skyhawks to the test.** *Above:* **The 'camel humps' on these A-4M Skyhawk IIs are integral avionics/electronic countermeasures pods.**

Grumman A-6E Intruder

The Grumman A-6 Intruder *(above)* succeeded the A-4 Skyhawk and serves the US fleet as an electronics warfare aircraft as well as an attack bomber. The acronym, 'TRAM,' which is visible on the aircraft's wing and belly pods, stands for Target Recognition Attack Multisensor, which provides the pilot with images of sight-invisible targets.

Douglas A-4E (A4D-5) Skyhawk

Above: This cutaway of the Douglas A-4E Skyhawk without the camel hump electronics pod shows how they fit all the goodies into the rather small, trim frame of the Skyhawk, and still produce a very solid performer. The pink areas are fuel tanks. Note the arresting hook at rear, refueling probe at front, and the 20 mm cannon in the forward wing root. At 27 feet, six inches by 39 feet, four inches (41 feet, four inches in later Skyhawks), the Skyhawk is a very compact aircraft. The A-4E pictured here has a top speed of 673 mph clean, cruising speed of 498 mph, and a combat ceiling of 40,050 feet. The last model made was the A-4M. Skyhawks continue service in US Navy reserve, training and utility units.

After World War II, with the strategic nuclear strike role in mind, the Navy began to develop a series of heavy attack bombers in the same size and weight class as Air Force medium bombers. Designed to be as big and heavy as possible while still being able to operate from a carrier deck, these aircraft included the propeller-driven North American AJ Savage, which first flew in 1948, and the twin jet Douglas A3D Skywarrior, which first flew in 1952. Retired from its intended role, the A3D (A-3 after 1962) continued in service into the 1980s as an electronic warfare aircraft and aerial refueling tanker.

The first major Navy postwar fighter was the Grumman F8F Bearcat. First flown in 1944, the Bearcat arrived in service too late for World War II. Embodying the best of Grumman's wartime 'carrier-cat' legacy, the F8F was considered by many to have been one of the best propeller-driven fighters ever built. In 1946 it was the Navy's top fighter, but by 1949 it had been replaced by jets. Thus, by fluke, one of the best fighters of all time just barely missed serving in either World War II or Korea. Bearcats today remain popular contenders on the civilian air race circuit, where they consistently trade propeller-craft world speed records with P-51 Mustangs.

The Navy's first jet fighter flew on 26 January 1945. Designated FH and nicknamed Phantom, it was the second airplane built by a relative newcomer to the field—McDonnell Aircraft of St Louis, Missouri. Started before the war by James Smith McDonnell, this small company won the contract with an extraordinary stroke of luck, but soon proved itself worthy. McDonnell went on to become one of the most important builders of jet fighter planes in the postwar world. The immediate successor to the Phantom was the F2H Banshee, which first flew in 1947 and which served with great distinction in

Below: The Douglas A-3 Skywarrior eventually traded its carrier-based bomber role for either one of two: electronics warfare aircraft or aerial refueling tanker. *Above:* The McDonnell FH-1 Phantom was the Navy's first jet. *At right:* Over Greece, an F2H Banshee prepares to return to its carrier, the USS *Midway*, in March of 1952.

Korea. The Banshee was followed by the swept-wing F3H Demon, which first flew in 1951 and which served with the Fleet until the early 1960s.

By far the most important McDonnell fighter for the Navy, and perhaps the most important American jet fighter in the postwar era, began life as an attack plane. Originally designated AH, the McDonnell Phantom II was completed as the F4H. Making its first flight on 27 May 1958, the F4H (F-4 after 1962) was the largest fighter in the Navy. It was also unusual for its two-man crew. Unlike most fighters, the Phantom II carried both a pilot and a weapons system operator.

In the finest tribute that might be paid to a Navy fighter, the Air Force decided in 1962 that it, too, would buy the Phantom II. During the Vietnam War it was the top fighter in service with both the Air Force and the Marine Corps, as well as the Navy. The definitive war era Navy version was the F-4B, which was joined in 1966 by the more advanced F-4J. The Navy and Air Force Phantoms accounted for more victories in air-to-air combat in Southeast Asia than all other types combined. All of the American aces in the war flew Phantoms, including the team of Navy lieutenants Randy Cunningham and Willie Driscoll, who were the first—as well as the highest—scoring American aces in Vietnam with six victories each.

Above: Being 'set' on a catapult aboard the USS *Coral Sea* is an F3H McDonnell Demon.
Below: The F4H McDonnell Phantom II was a legendary 'bomb truck' as well as having been the top US Air Force, US Marine and US Navy fighter in the Vietnam conflict.

Above right: Phantoms with missiles; note the empty missile rack on the near plane. The F-4 Phantom II is America's most widely used supersonic combat plane, and is considered the best fighter-bomber ever built. *Below right:* Carrier-based Phantoms head home.

McDonnell's F2H Banshee typified Navy carrier fighters in Korea, and their F-4 Phantom did the same in Vietnam, but in the intervening years a number of other important aircraft graced the decks of American carriers. These included the North American FJ Fury (Naval equivalent of the F-86 Sabre jet), which entered service in 1948; the Douglas F3D Skyknight, which entered service with the Navy and Marine Corps as a night fighter in 1950; the Vought F7U Cutlass that entered service in 1953; and the Douglas F4D Skyray, a Delta-winged fighter that joined the Navy in 1953 as a fleet defense interceptor. In 1957 and again in 1958, a Skyray-equipped squadron was named as the top interceptor squadron in the North American Air Defense Command (NORAD), even though it was the only Navy unit assigned to that Air Force dominated command. The Skyray remained in production until 1958 and retired from service in 1964, six months prior to the Vietnam War.

Having built some of the Navy's best fighters during World War II, Grumman embarked on a postwar program of jet fighters. The first of these, the XF9F-1, was ordered in April 1946, canceled in October and replaced by the XF9F-2, which first flew on 24 November 1947 with the nickname

Panther. A large number of these straight-winged fighters were in service with both Navy and Marine Corps squadrons by the Korean War.

The second Grumman jet fighter, the Cougar, was actually born as a swept-wing variation on the Panther. The prototype was an F9F-5 with new wings retrofitted. The first production Cougars, designated F9F-6, joined the fleet in December 1951 but only a handful arrived in Korea before the war ended in 1953. The F10F designation went to an experimental fighter with variable-sweep wings that Grumman delivered in 1952, but which was canceled as impractical after early tests. Thus, the next Grumman production jet fighter was the F11F Tigercat, which first flew in 1954. Like its contemporary, the Douglas Skyray, the Tigercat arrived on the heels of the Korean War, but was retired before it saw combat in Vietnam.

Second only to the McDonnell F-4 in combat in Vietnam was the Vought F-8 (F8U before 1962) Crusader. It first flew in March 1955 and was in service two years later. In service aboard the Navy's USS *Essex*-class aircraft carriers, the Crusader accounted for more aerial victories than any other aircraft except the Phantom, earning it the nickname 'MiG-Master.'

US Navy Postwar Fighters

Specifications[*]	Grumman F8F Bearcat	Douglas F4D Skyray	Grumman F9F Cougar	Vought F8U(F-8) Crusader	McDonnell F4H(F-4) Phantom II
First Flight[*]	1944	1951	1951	1955	1958
Wing span	35'6"	33'6"	34'6"	35'8"	38'5"
Length	27'8"	45'8"	40'11"	54'3"	58'3"
Gross weight	10,426 lb	26,000 lb	18,450 lb	27,810 lb	43,907 lb
Top speed	447 mph	723 mph	654 mph	1105 mph	1490 mph
Range	1435 mi	593 mi	932 mi	1490 mi	1297 mi
Engine	Pratt & Whitney R2800 (1 radial)	Pratt & Whitney J57 (1 turbojet)	Pratt & Whitney J48 (1 turbojet)	Pratt & Whitney J75 (1 turbojet)	General Electric J79 (2 turbojet)
Engine rating	1975 hp	16,000 lb thrust	6250 lb thrust	10,700 lb thrust	17,000 lb thrust

[*] First Flight is for series prototype, data is for F8F-2, F4D-1, F9F-6, F-8C, and F-4B

Below left: Grumman F9F Cougars head for their carrier home, the USS *Bon Homme Richard,* after a strike at North Korean military targets in the early 1950s. *Below:* Douglas F4D Skyrays of US Navy Fighter Squadron 74 dominate this airfield photo. In the background, however, there are a few Douglas A4D Skyhawks, Douglas A3D Skywarriors and Vought F8U Crusaders. *Above:* So you want to be a carrier pilot, eh? An airborne view of an F4D Skyray going in for a landing on the seemingly tiny flight deck of the USS *Essex.*

Above: Early Crusaders carried internally-mounted rocket pods of 32 rockets each, but when these pods were lowered for firing, the aircraft pitched upward, interfering with accuracy—as a consequence, the rocket pods were replaced with the Sidewinder missile racks seen on this plane. *Above left:* An F-8 comes in for a landing on the USS *John F Kennedy.* Note the variable-incidence wing panel, tilted upward here for air braking.

Vought (LTV) F-8H Crusader and A-7E Corsair II

Above: A flight of Vought A-7E Corsair IIs. The A-7 Corsair was derived from the F8U Crusader for the role of close-support ground attack aircraft. In Vietnam, early Corsair models performed many tasks including flying support for demanding search and rescue missions. Basically the same airframe as the Crusader, the Corsair is built to haul heavy munitions loads. One capability of the Corsair is as an all-weather strike fighter. The A-7E Corsair has armament specification for one 20 mm Vulcan electric cannon and maximum external stores of 20,000 pounds. The A-7D Corsair had the lowest mission abort rate of any aircraft in the Vietnam conflict, losing only four aircraft to enemy fire in over 6000 sorties. While the Crusader fighter topped out at 1120 mph, the slow but deadly Corsair bomb truck tops out at 633 mph with 12,250 pounds of bombs aboard. Since 1973, A-7s that had been active with the USAF have been turned over to the Air National Guard in 11 states and Puerto Rico. The A-7 had an outstanding target strike record in Southeast Asia. *At left:* A cutaway view of the Vought F-8 Crusader.

POSTWAR US AIR FORCE BOMBERS

When the US Air Force was established in September 1947, most of the vast wartime inventory of more than 20,000 USAAF bombers had been scrapped. Only 2112 Boeing B-29s remained, but a new generation of long-range bombers was taking shape in the Air Force's plan for its future. Most notable was the six-engined Convair B-36 Peacemaker. The largest strategic bomber ever built, it represented the epitome of World War II era thinking about bombers. It was not fast, but it had a huge bomb capacity and a very long range. Originally planned during the war, the B-36 was postponed and made its first flight on 8 August 1946. As the big bombers entered service with the Strategic Air Command in the late 1940s, their lack of speed became a concern, so B-36Bs were retrofitted with underwing jet engine pods beginning in 1949. These in turn became standard on all B-36 models through the B-36J, the last of which were delivered in 1953.

The B-36 served in SAC through 12 February 1959 without ever having been in combat. It did, however, become involved in a number of interesting projects beyond simply being in the front line of American nuclear deterrent for more than a decade. These included the FICON (Fighter-Conveyor) project of 1951-55 in which the Air Force experimented with carrying F-84s and F-85s *aboard* B-36s to serve as fighter escorts. Ultimately FICON was abandoned as impractical. Another project, conducted in 1955, involved a Peacemaker designated NB-36H, which was the first aircraft to carry a functioning nuclear reactor. The reactor, although it did not supply motive power to the airplane in this test, was intended to be the prototype for those that *could* be used to power aircraft. This project was also abandoned as impractical.

In addition to the huge B-36, the Air Force also bought a number of all-jet medium bombers. Notable among these were the North American B-45 Tornado and the Boeing B-47 Stratojet. The latter was the first swept-wing American bomber and it also has the distinction of having been produced in larger numbers (2040) than any American bomber since World War II. Born in

continued on page 116

Above: This photo illustrates the huge appetite of the Convair B-36 Peacemaker bomber: all of these trucks were needed to supply the behemoth with its 21,116 gallons of gasoline and 1200 gallons of oil. *Above opposite:* The North American B-45 Tornado medium bomber design applied jet propulsion to World War II-era bomber design techniques—the B-45 served in Korea and in peacetime Europe. *At right:* The Boeing B-47 Stratojet bomber served the USAF until 1966, with one RB-47 reconnaissance version serving until 1967.

These pages: The symbol of US strategic military power in the 1950s was the Boeing B-52 Stratofortress. The first flights of the XB-52 prototype and the YB-52 service test aircraft came in 1952. Both of these aircraft had been designed with a fighter-style cockpit (such as had been used on the B-47), but General Curtis LeMay, commander of the US Air Force Strategic Air Command, insisted that it be redesigned with side-by-side seating for pilot and co-pilot such as had been conventional on all preceding American heavy bombers. This design was incorporated on the B-52A and all subsequent Stratofortresses. (See chart on page 119).

The first production model B-52A was delivered in 1954, followed by the B-52B series—which consisted primarily of RB-52B reconnaissance aircraft—and the B-52C and B-52D series aircraft which were heavier and had more fuel capacity. The B-52E (seen in the photo *above*) had improved avionics, while the B-52F had more powerful turbojet engines.

All of the Stratofortresses through the B-52E had the trademark tall tail clearly seen in this photo, while the more advanced B-52G and B-52H had redesigned wings and shorter tail planes *(see following pages)*. The ultimate Stratofortress, the B-52H, was powered by turbofan (rather than turbojet) engines, giving it greatly enhanced performance.

continued from page 112

the depths of the Cold War, the huge B-47 production program was a result of the perceived threat of Soviet attack and the need to strike back. The B-47 wasn't designed with the intercontinental range of the B-36, but bases in Europe and aerial refueling helped address this shortcoming.

The B-47 first flew in 1947, entered service with the Strategic Air Command in 1951, and remained in production until 1957 and in service until 1966. An electronic reconnaissance version (RB-47H), introduced in 1955, remained in service until 1967 and was the only Stratojet to make an appearance during the Vietnam War.

Of the great bombers produced in the postwar world, one stands out. The Boeing B-52 Stratofortress was almost as sleek as the B-47, almost as big as the B-36 and it had the speed, range and durability to outfly either of them. Developed as an all-jet successor to the B-36, it combined the swept wings of the B-47 with a capacity that easily put it in the heavy bomber class. It was first flown in 1951 and entered service three years later. During the 1950s the B-52 evolved as the centerpiece of the Strategic Air Command's strategic deterrent. As a demonstration of the big bomber's prowess, the Strategic Air Command undertook operation *Power Flight*, a January 1957 exercise in which three B-52s flew nonstop (with aerial refueling) around the world in 45 hours 19 minutes, averaging 530 mph over the 24,325 miles. On 10 January 1962, another B-52 took off from Kadena AFB on Okinawa, and flew nonstop and *without refueling* 12,532 miles to Madrid, setting a world distance record.

Above: A B-52D cruises along a wooded coastline. The manned tail turret seen here was replaced with a robot turret in models beginning with the B-52G. *Below:* A B-52 and a B-47 cruise together near Eglin Air Force Base in Florida. *At right:* A test flight of the experimental Northrop YB-49 Flying Wing bomber—it carried 10,000 pounds of bombs.

The last of 744 Stratofortresses, a B-52H, was delivered three years later in 1965. After a decade of service, the Stratofortress was finally used in combat for the first time. Beginning 18 June 1965, SAC B-52s based at Andersen AFB on Guam, and later at U Tapao Royal Thai Naval Air Base, were used to bomb enemy targets in the jungles of South Vietnam. Designated *Arc Light,* these raids expended enormous amounts of ordnance on targets of questionable tactical importance.

It was not until December 1972 that the big bombers were put to work on strategic targets in North Vietnam. Between 18 December and 29 December, the strategic air offensive against North Vietnam's capital and major port, which was designated *Linebacker II,* saw as many as 120 B-52s launched on a single night. The result of these raids was that North Vietnam pleaded for a ceasefire at the Paris peace talks. It took two years after the Americans withdrew for the communists to rebuild the war machine to the level required for another major offensive. After the war, the Stratofortresses continued to be SAC's leading strategic bomber, outliving a number of proposed replacements.

The B-52D subtype was the most used variant during the war, having been modified to carry 27 tons of bombs, triple the capacity of other subtypes. It was the only one of the high-tailed early models (B-52A through B-52F) to be retained in service after the war. The B-52F, which had been used in the early days, was retired upon completion of the B-52D bomb bay modification program. When the B-52D was finally retired in 1984, this left over 300

continued on page 122

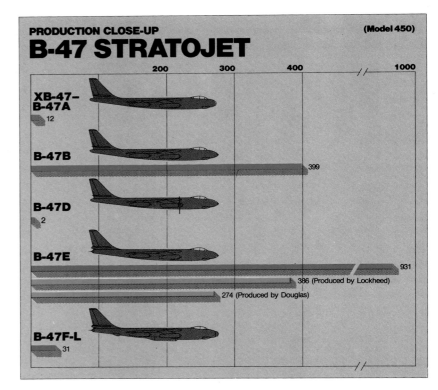

PRODUCTION CLOSE-UP (Model 450)
B-47 STRATOJET

PRODUCTION CLOSE-UP
B-52 STRATOFORTRESS
(Model 464)

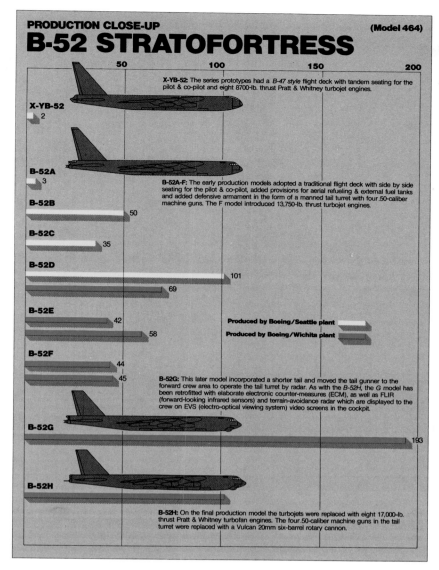

X-YB-52: The series prototypes had a *B-47 style* flight deck with tandem seating for the pilot & co-pilot and eight 8700-lb. thrust Pratt & Whitney turbojet engines.

X-YB-52 — 2

B-52A — 3

B-52A-F: The early production models adopted a traditional flight deck with side by side seating for the pilot & co-pilot, added provisions for aerial refueling & external fuel tanks and added defensive armament in the form of a manned tail turret with four .50-caliber machine guns. The F model introduced 13,750-lb. thrust turbojet engines.

B-52B — 50

B-52C — 35

B-52D — 101 / 69

B-52E — 42 / 58

Produced by Boeing/Seattle plant
Produced by Boeing/Wichita plant

B-52F — 44 / 45

B-52G: This later model incorporated a shorter tail and moved the tail gunner to the forward crew area to operate the tail turret by radar. As with the *B-52H*, the G model has been retrofitted with elaborate electronic counter-measures (ECM), as well as FLIR (forward-looking infrared sensors) and terrain-avoidance radar which are displayed to the crew on EVS (electro-optical viewing system) video screens in the cockpit.

B-52G — 193

B-52H

B-52H: On the final production model the turbojets were replaced with eight 17,000-lb. thrust Pratt & Whitney turbofan engines. The four .50-caliber machine guns in the tail turret were replaced with a Vulcan 20mm six-barrel rotary cannon.

Opposite: A twilight launch takes a B-52D over a partially-completed Buddhist temple near the U Tapao air base in Thailand. *Above:* A B-52D unloads its ordnance. *Below:* A load of 1000- and 750-pound bombs is dispensed near Bien Hoa AB, in Vietnam, on 1 December 1968.

119

Postwar US Air Force Bombers

Specifications[*]	Convair B-36 Peacemaker	Boeing B-47 Stratojet	Boeing B-52 Stratofortress	Convair B-58 Hustler	North American B-70 Valkyrie
Type	Heavy	Medium	Heavy	Medium	Heavy
First Flight[*]	1946	1947	1952	1956	1964
Wing span	230'	116'	185'	56'10"	105'
Length	162'	107'1"	156'	96'9"	185'
Gross weight	310,380 lb	198,180 lb	450,000 lb	163,000 lb	521,056 lb
Top speed	418 mph	607 mph	639 mph	1321 mph	1982 mph
Range	9440 mi	4035 mi	11,000 mi	5028 mi	4290 mi
Engine	(a)Pratt & Whitney R4360 (6) (b) General Electric J47 (4)	General Electric J47 (6)	Pratt & Whitney TF33 (8)	General Electric J79 (4)	General Electric YJ93 (6)
Engine rating	(a) 3800 hp (b) 5200 lb thrust	5970 lb thrust	17,000 lb thrust	10,300 lb thrust	28,000 lb thrust

[*] First flights are for prototypes, data is for B-36J, B-47E, B-52H, B-58A and XB-70.

At top, above: A test flight of the XB-70 Valkyrie over Edwards AFB on 3 November 1965; note the B-58 Hustler chase plane. *Above:* The Mach 2 Convair B-58 Hustler, *(above)* was a great airplane, but was withdrawn from service in the 1960s by Defense Secretary Robert McNamara amid great controversy.

B-52G and B-52H aircraft that had been extensively modernized and remodeled with elaborate electronic gear and terrain-following radar. Both the turbojet-powered B-52G and the turbofan-powered B-52H are equipped to carry conventional bombs (the B-52G was used in Vietnam) or nuclear weapons. Many of both types have also been modified to carry AGM-86 Air Launched Cruise Missiles.

The world's first supersonic bomber was the delta-winged Convair B-58 Hustler, which first flew in 1956 and which went into service with SAC in 1960 alongside the B-52. Designed to perform its mission at twice the speed of sound, the B-58 was, and will be, the fastest bomber to go into squadron service in the US Air Force in the 20th century. A total of 166 B-58s were built but they remained in service only through 1970. The reason that such a high performance aircraft should be retired after so short a career has been the subject of a great deal of speculation. The major factor was a theory that developed in the Defense Department in the 1960s that held that unmanned intercontinental ballistic missiles were more capable of performing the nuclear deterrent role than were manned bombers. The B-52 was retained while the B-58 was phased out because it was considered to be more versatile in the conventional role, as proven in Vietnam. The B-58 was also more difficult to maintain because its systems were state-of-the-art and extremely complex and sophisticated.

In the late 1950s, the Air Force considered building a bomber that could cruise at *three times* the speed of sound. In 1959, this ambitious program was canceled, but it was restored in 1960 as as a research project only. The result was the North American XB-70 Valkyrie, which first flew in 1964. Two of these huge aircraft were built and tested at Mach 3 before one of them was lost and the program was finally terminated in 1969.

At right: **North American Aviation's huge Mach 3 XB-70 takes off with an ear-shattering roar.** *Below:* **The Mach 2 Convair B-58 Hustler.** *Above:* **USAF ground crew members attach an Air Launched Cruise Missile (ALCM) pod to the underwing of a B-52G.** *At far right:* **The refueling boom of a KC-135 tanker connects with an ALCM-armed B-52G, whose nose bumps contain electronic sensors.**

While this chapter is devoted largely to medium and heavy bombers, mention should also be made of two important *light* bombers that evolved in the 1950s and which saw service in Vietnam in the 1960s. In the box *below* is the B-57 Canberra, aka 'Cranberry,' developed originally by English Electric, which was the first aircraft of non-US design to be adopted for service by the US military since 1918, due to the plane's ideal light bomber design. It was built by Martin under a licensing contract with the British.

In the main photo on these pages is the Douglas B-66B Destroyer, which was developed from the Navy's A-3 Skywarrior with much major alteration. The B-66 was the only Destroyer variant which was exclusively a bomber; it could carry both conventional and nuclear stores—a B-66B took part in operation Redwing, which was the hydrogen bomb drop on Bikini Atoll. The aircraft of the EB-66E Destroyer variant served as radar jammers and intelligence gatherers in Vietnam, and were withdrawn from service in 1974.

POSTWAR US AIR FORCE FIGHTERS

By the end of World War II, Germany had put its first jet fighters into combat and both the United States and Britain had jet fighters that were very nearly ready for their baptism of fire. The war ended before this could happen, but the focus in immediate postwar fighter development was on jets. Every major aircraft manufacturer that had built important USAAF fighters during the war had a jet fighter program rolling before the war ended.

Lockheed, which built the war era P-38 Lightning, first flew its P-80 Shooting Star on 1 June 1944, and the USAAF had just gotten it into squadron service at the end of the war.

Republic, which had produced the great P-47 Thunderbolt during the war, was working on the P-84 Thunderjet by war's end and had it in the air in February 1946.

Curtiss, which built the P-40 Warhawk that served so well at the beginning of the war, attempted to get into the field but only a simple example of their P-87 Blackhawk was built. It flew in March 1948 but the project was canceled, ending a long line of Curtiss warplanes that dated back to the dawn of aviation history.

North American, which had produced the P-51 Mustang, the top USAAF fighter during the war, went on to produce the F-86 Sabre Jet, the most important jet fighter produced in the west for a quarter century.

When the US Air Force was established in 1947 and the 'P' for pursuit designation was changed to 'F' for fighter, the F-80 Shooting Star was the leading operational fighter, with the F-84 Thunderjet coming close on its heels. Both were straight-winged fighters designed in an era before the

Above left: A flight of Lockheed F-80 Shooting Stars. Captain Ralph Parr claimed 10 aerial victories with his F-80C Shooting Star during the Korean War. *Below:* A row of Republic F-84 Thunderstreaks on an Alaskan airfield—the F-84F Thunderstreak was the swept-wing variant of the straight-wing F-84 Thunderjet, and was also the first single-seat fighter-bomber capable of carrying a tactical nuclear weapon. *Above:* Brand-new F-80s in all-metal finish await their pilots in the early 1950s.

aerodynamic importance of swept wings on high-speed aircraft was fully understood. In 1949, Republic began experimenting with the idea of a swept-wing F-84, and when the Korean War started in June 1950 they were given a contract to start producing them under the designation F-84F.

Both the F-80 and F-84 were used in the Korean War, with an F-80 emerging victorious from the first jet-to-jet air battle in history on 8 November 1950. With the arrival of the swept-wing F-86, the role for the two straight-winged types in air-to-air combat diminished, but they both remained in combat for the duration. The F-84, like its older brother the P-47 in World War II, served as a durable fighter-bomber, dropping 55,987 tons of bombs.

The great F-86 Sabre Jet actually began life under a US Navy contract of 1 January 1945 that called for a straight-winged jet fighter to be developed under the XFJ designation. The USAAF joined the project in May, designating their version XP-86.

An XP-86 mock-up was delivered to the USAAF on 20 June 1945, but even then North American engineers thought that the standard straight-wing configuration might be obsolete. Theoretical studies on swept wings in Germany dating back to 1940 had postulated that swept wings could greatly enhance an aircraft's performance as it approached the speed of sound. Since those speeds were still considered impossible, the idea of swept wings attracted little attention outside Germany. Within the Reich, however, a number of swept-wing designs evolved hand-in-hand with the advent of jet engines. The Messerschmitt Me262, the most widely used jet fighter of the war, was designed with slightly swept wings and these had added greatly to its performance.

As time went on, jet fighters took on a more streamlined appearance. *Above* is a straight-wing F-84 Thunderjet (note the 364 Korean War combat mission hash marks on this plane's fuselage), and *below* is the first F-84 swept-wing Thunderstreak. *At right,* to carry the theme a step further, is the epochal North American F-86 Sabre Jet.

Postwar US Air Force Fighters

Specifications[*]	Lockheed F-80 Shooting Star	Republic F-84 Thunderjet	North American F-86 Sabre Jet	Northrop F-89 Scorpion	Lockheed F-94 Starfire
Primary Function	Fighter	Fighter-Bomber	Fighter	Interceptor	Interceptor
First Flight[*]	1944	1946	1947	1948	1949
Wing span	39'11'	36'5"	37'1"	56'	37'4"
Length	34'6"	38'6"	37'6"	53'6"	44'6"
Gross weight	11,700 lb	22,463	15,876	37,348	20,825
Top speed	580 mph	613 mph	679 mph	650 mph	640 mph
Range	1380 mi	1950 mi	1052 mi	905 mi	1275 mi
Engine	Allison J33 (1)	Allison J35 (1)	General Electric J47 (1)	Allison J35 (2)	Pratt & Whitney J-48 (1)
Engine thrust	4600 lb	4900 lb	5200 lb	5600 lb	6350 lb

* First flights are fore series prototypes, data is for F-80C, F-84E, F-86A, F-89C and F-94C.

North American Aviation F-86 Sabre Jet

In the spring of 1948, the prototype F-86 became the first US fighter to break the speed of sound, during a shallow dive. In 1949, the F-86 set a new air speed record of 671 mph. The basic F-86A was followed in production by an interceptor model, the F-86D 'Sabre Dog', with a slatted wing and a reworked tail. This and the F-86F had much success in the Korean War, and established a 10 to one combat kill dominion over the faster MiG-15s. The gunless F-86D was equipped with rockets, afterburner, autopilot and radar for collision course interception attack; and the F-86K was equipped with guns as well as the rocket firing system. Considered by many to 'top the list' was the F-86H model, with a top speed of 692 mph, a service ceiling of 50,800 feet and a combat radius of 519 miles.

The fighter that won the air war in Korea: *In the box, opposite:* An F-86 Sabre Jet slices the air above the cloud tops. Note the flash burns on this fighter's nose gun ports. *Below:* A cutaway view of the North American F-86 Sabre Jet. The F-86E Sabre was the first truly great jet fighter. Various radar and avionics packages caused its nose configuration to change somewhat between models (see pages 132-133), but the basic Sabre Jet greatness was there in all models.

As the war in Europe ended in May, North American's Chief Engineer Raymond Rice and P-86 Project Aerodynamicist L P Greene got their hands on some Me262 data and decided to transform the P-86 into a swept-wing fighter. This modification, approved on 1 November 1945, proved to be the most important part of the project, as it transformed the P-86 from just another jet plane into what would become the world's first truly great jet fighter. The difference can be proven by comparing the P-86 (F-86 after 1948) to the Navy's early FJ-series fighters that grew from the same roots, but retained the straight wings.

The XFJ-1 first flew on 11 September 1946, and first underwent aircraft carrier trials aboard the USS *Boxer* in March 1948. The first swept-wing XP-86 'Sabre' was delivered to the USAAF on 10 September 1947, eight days before that service became the fully independent US Air Force. The first flight of this prototype came on the first of October. On 26 April 1948, the first prototype broke the sound barrier for the first time, although there is some evidence to support the unconfirmed rumors that it actually exceeded Mach 1 prior to Chuck Yeager's official first-ever supersonic flight of 14 October 1947. Though technically a supersonic fighter, the Air Force restricted the aircraft to Mach .95 (668 mph) below 25,000 feet.

With the basic F-86A proving to be such an outstanding fighter, the Air Force proceeded with plans to adapt it for other roles. First of these was the NA-157, a long-range escort fighter version ordered under the designation F-93 (originally F-86C) and the NA-164 interceptor version ordered under the designation F-95. First flown on 25 January 1950, the YF-93A had a solid nose and fuselage-side intakes, but in other respects it resembled the F-86A upon which it was based. A total of 120 F-93s were ordered but only two flight test aircraft were built due to cuts in the Air Force's long-range fighter program budget.

When the Korean War began on 25 June 1950, the Mustangs and straight-winged Lockheed F-80 jet fighters that the US Air Force initially deployed were more than adequate to handle the rag-tag inventory of aging aircraft in the inventory of the North Korean air force. On 1 November, however, the situation changed dramatically when Russian-built swept-wing MiG-15 jet fighters appeared. An F-80C downed a MiG in history's first all-jet air combat on 8 November, but generally the MiG-15s outclassed anything that the US Air Force had in Korea. On that same day the F-86-equipped Fourth Fighter Interceptor Squadron was ordered to Korea. The Fourth was picked because it had a large number of pilots with a great deal of air-to-air combat experience in World War II.

In the five weeks that it took the F-86s to be shipped to Korea, the Chinese Communists began a major land offensive, while their MiG-15s seized the air superiority over the battlefield from the Americans.

The Sabres arrived at Kimpo AB near Seoul, South Korea on 13 December and met the enemy for the first time four days later. Four F-86As encountered four Chinese MiG-15s over North Korea, downing one and chasing the others across the Yalu River into China.

During those 32 months in MiG Alley the F-86 Sabres of the USAF Fifth Air Force flew 87,177 sorties, or individual per-plane missions. This amounted to roughly 22 four-plane patrols per day, a pretty good rate, considering that the average number of Sabres was 184 at any given time. By the end of the year, the Fifth Air Force Sabres flew 236 sorties in December 1950, averaged 1024 per month for 1951 (including February when only *one* was flown due to the bases being overrun); 3279 for 1952 and 5045 per month for the first seven months of 1953.

The last three months of the war—May through July 1953—saw the three highest numbers of sorties: 6721, 7696 and 5841, respectively. June 1953 also saw 77 MiGs shot down, the highest score of any month of the war. In second place was September 1952 when 63 MiGs were downed.

In total, the Sabres shot down 792 MiGs (96 percent of the MiGs downed by American aircraft) and 18 aircraft of other types. There were 78 Sabres shot down in aerial combat with the MiGs, giving the F-86 a clear 10 to 1 superiority over the Soviet-built fighters. In addition to the 792 confirmed kills, the F-86s scored 118 probables and damaged another 814 enemy aircraft.

The new and improved subseries F-86F went into service with US Air Force units in both the United States and Korea in June 1952. In the midst of production it was discovered that if an extended leading edge replaced the slatted leading edge of the wing the F-86F could make much tighter turns at high altitudes, redressing one of the advantages that the MiG-15 had over Sabres. This change was made on the F-86Fs that were still at the factory and kits were sent to Korea in sufficient numbers to completely retrofit all the F-86Fs in the field.

Another F-86F field modification came in March 1953 when the six .50 caliber machine guns on eight aircraft were replaced with two to four 20mm cannons. The belt-fed cannons worked well in combat and eventually became

Above: A North American Sabre Jet releases one of its five-inch high velocity rockets in a weapons test over the Nellis AFB target range, in the 1950s. *At right,* left and right: An F-86D interceptor and a YF-93 (originally F-86C) long-range escort fighter, with a B-45 Tornado in the background. *Below:* An F-86F Sabre Jet at rest under a clear sky.

generally standard on the subsequent F-86H series and North American's later F-100 Super Sabre fighter.

The first F-86D 'Sabre Dog' interceptor variant joined the Air Force in March 1951 where it was intended for service with the Air Defense Command and never intended for use in Korea. Much faster than the other ADC interceptors—the Northrop F-89 and Lockheed F-94—the F-86D was operational with most ADC squadrons by 1955.

The final Sabre in the F-86D lineage, the F-86L, was not a new plane at all. Rather, it was a series of F-86Ds that were upgraded by North American and redelivered to the Air Force beginning in October 1956. The upgrading included the AN/APR-34 Data Link receiver and AN/APX-25 identification radar. By this time, the F-102 and F-106 interceptors were replacing the Dogs in Air Defense Command service, so most of the F-86Ls were delivered ultimately to the Air National Guard where they served until 1962.

In addition to the F-86D, the principal all-weather interceptors in the first generation of Air Force interceptors were the Northrop F-89 Scorpion and the Lockheed F-94 Starfire. Both were two-place aircraft with sophisticated electronic systems for flying and finding enemy aircraft in any kind of weather. They evolved as straight-winged fighters because their mission was to hunt bombers and kill them with missiles at long distances, so speed and maneuverability weren't as critical. The huge F-89 first flew in August 1948 and went into service in June 1951. The F-94 first flew in July 1949 and went into service in May 1950. The Scorpion remained in service through 1968, but the Starfire was retired in 1960.

A treasury of the great US Air Force interceptors of the 1950s. Note the black radomes in every nose of every plane on this page. Note also the 'Mighty Mouse' missile pods inboard of the wingtip fuel tanks of the Lockheed F-94 Starfire *below. Above:* The F-86D Sabre. *At right:* Northrop F-89 Scorpions, the USAF's first all-weather capable fighters.

The second generation of US Air Force jet fighters were the group known as the 'century series' because their numbering began at F-100. The North American F-100 Super Sabre, as its name implies, was intended originally as a successor to the F-86 as an air superiority fighter. It exceeded the speed of sound on its first flight on 25 May 1953. The definitive versions were the F-100C fighter, which entered service in 1955, and the F-100D fighter-bomber, which entered service in 1956. The latter went on to serve in the war in Southeast Asia from August 1964 through July 1971.

The second century series fighter was the McDonnell F-101 Voodoo, a long-range fighter originally designed to escort SAC's long-range bombers. It was, however, delivered to the Tactical Air Command as a fighter-bomber instead. First flown in 1952, the F-101 served in TAC from 1957 through 1966. The interceptor version, the F-101B, was originally assigned to the Air Defense Command in 1957 and it continued to serve in the US Air Force through 1966 and with the US National Guard and the Canadian armed forces into the 1980s. Reconnaissance versions, RF-101A and RF-101C, were introduced to Southeast Asia in 1961 and continued to serve until 1970.

The Convair F-102 Delta Dagger interceptor was the first delta-winged jet fighter to go into *service* with the US Air Force, although it was preceded by, and indeed based upon, Convair's purely experimental XF-92. The latter first flew in 1948 and provided valuable information for the design of the Delta Dagger, which first flew in January 1954. The F-102 'Deuce,' as it came to be known, became operational with the Air Defense Command in 1956, where it remained in service until 1974. Strictly an interceptor, the F-102's service in Vietnam consisted of only a brief tour in 1964 when there was a perceived threat of North Vietnamese bombing attacks on American installations in Southeast Asia.

The design of the Lockheed F-104 Starfighter was based on the experiences of combat pilots in the Korean War and their need for a very fast, maneuverable air superiority fighter that could function well at high altitudes. First flown in February 1956, it established several speed and altitude records, thus living up to its promise in this regard. In service, however, the F-104 left much to be desired because it lacked range and load-carrying ability. Despite this, it was adopted in the 1960s by Germany and a number of other NATO nations as their standard multipurpose fighter. Its high accident rate in this period reached crisis proportions in Europe and earned the Starfighter a reputation as a 'widow maker.' As pilot proficiency increased, however, the accident rate plummeted. Now considered a reliable aircraft, the F-104 continued to serve in many European air forces into the 1980s.

Above: A family portrait of the USAF's 'century' series, clockwise from the bottom: the Lockheed F-104 Starfighter; the North American F-100 Super Sabre (which service designation started the century series); the Convair F-102 Delta Dagger; the McDonnell F-101 Voodoo; and the Republic F-105 Thunderchief. Missing from this photo are the latter two century series fighters, the Convair F-106 Delta Dart and the North American F-107 *Super* Super Sabre—both of which are pictured on the following pages. *Below:* An F-102 Delta Dagger in flight. *At right:* F-100C Super Sabres slice the sky.

136

US Air Force Century Series Fighters

Specifications*	North American F-100 Super Sabre	McDonnell F-101 Voodoo	Lockheed F-104 Starfighter	Republic F-105 Thunderchief	Convair F-106 Delta Dart
Primary Function	Fighter/Fighter-bomber	Interceptor/Fighter	Fighter	Fighter-bomber	Interceptor
First Flight*	1953	1954	1954	1955	1956**
Wing span	38'10"	39'8"	21'11"	34'11"	38'2"
Length	47'10"	67'5"	54'9"	64'5"	70'9"
Gross weight	32,615 lb	48,001 lb	22,614 lb	48,976 lb	34,510 lb
Top speed	924 mph	1005 mph	1324 mph	1372 mph	1328 mph
Range	1954 mi	2186 mi	1585 mi	2208 mi	1809 mi
Engine	Pratt & Whitney J57 turbojet (1)	Pratt & Whitney J57 turbojet (2)	Pratt & Whitney J79 turbojet (1)	Pratt & Whitney J75 turbojet (1)	Pratt & Whitney J75 turbojet (1)
Engine thrust	10,200 lb	10,200 lb	9600 lb	16,100 lb	16,100 lb

* First flights are for series prototypes, other data is for F-100C, F-101A, F-104A, F-105D and F-106A.

** The F-106A was a development of the F-102B. The F-102 first flew in 1953.

While the F-104 was conceived as a high performance air superiority fighter that wound up as a fighter-bomber, the Republic F-105 Thunderchief was *designed* as a fighter-bomber that wound up with 27.5 victories in air-to-air combat. The F-105 was conceived as a successor to Republic's earlier successful fighter-bombers, the P-47 and F-84. It first flew in October 1955 and went into service in 1958. The first F-105 combat mission was flown against North Vietnam on 2 March 1965 and it became the most used aircraft of its type in the war. The 'Thud,' as it was known to pilots in Southeast Asia, served until the end of the war and continued in the Air Force until 1984.

The Convair F-106 Delta Dart was originally designated F-102B, but a sufficient number of changes were introduced to warrant an all-new designation. First flown in December 1956, this delta-winged interceptor went into service with the Air Defense Command in March 1959 and remained in production through July 1961. An extraordinarily reliable aircraft, the F-106 remained as the leading interceptor in the Air Force through the 1960s and 1970s and still served in both Air Force and Air National Guard squadrons through 1988. This record for longevity is unmatched by any other major Air Force fighter and is likely to be exceeded only by the F-4 Phantom.

Of the other fighters in the century series, the Republic F-103, North American F-108 and McDonnell F-109 were never built, and the North American F-107 'Super Super Sabre' was canceled in February 1957 after completion of three prototypes.

At right: A Republic F-105 Thunderchief plies the rosey cloudtops; the sizable 'Thud' could do 1372 mph. *Above:* An F-106 Delta Dart looses one of its AIM-4 Falcon air-to-air missiles (AAMs), and *below right,* three Darts fly past Alaska's Denali (once aka Mt McKinley). *Below:* The last F-105 in USAF service, in 1983. *Far right:* The F-107 *Super* Super Sabre.

After the century series came the McDonnell F-110 Phantom, which became the F-4, and the General Dynamics F-111. The F-111 was based on a 1961 Defense Department quest for a fighter-bomber with variable sweep wings that could be used by both the Air Force and the Navy. Designated as the Tactical Fighter Experimental (TFX), the new aircraft was intended to be economical because the two services would not be buying two different airplanes. However, because Navy and Air Force requirements were so dissimilar, the plane tried to be all things to all people, resulting in a design that was so drastically compromised that the Navy dropped out of the TFX program altogether.

The first F-111 flew in December 1964 and production aircraft were introduced into combat in Southeast Asia in March 1968. Loss rates were initially so high that the planes had to be withdrawn for modifications to their terrain-following radar systems. In September 1972, the 'Aardvarks,' as they were now known, were reintroduced to combat in Southeast Asia, where they were extremely successful. The F-111 continued to serve in the Air Force after the war, with a large number assigned to Europe for potential long-range low-level attacks behind Warsaw Pact lines if war should break out in this theater. In April 1986, F-111s based in England conducted strikes against terrorist bases in northern Libya.

Perhaps the most successful Air Force fighter since World War II was the McDonnell F-4 Phantom, which was born as a Navy attack plane (*see Chapter Eight*). Having evolved as a fighter, the Phantom first flew in May 1958 under the designation F4H, entering service with the Navy in 1961. In 1962 the Air Force announced that it would also be buying Phantoms, giving them the designation F-110. Later in the year the Navy and Air Force nomenclature

Above, **left and right: Captain Steve Ritchie and Captain Chuck Debellevue, two of the three USAF aces of the Vietnam War (the third was Captain Jefferey Feinstein), are shown in this October 1972 photo as they stand beside their F-4, which is decorated with five red stars—one star for each MiG 'bagged.'** *Below:* **A sharkfaced USAF F-4E totes its burden of grief toward a Vietnamese target in 1970.** *Above right:* **A Northrop F-5A Freedom Fighter, loaded for bear.** *Below right:* **A General Dynamics F-111F 'Aardvark.'**

Third Generation US Air Force Fighters

Specifications*	General Dynamics F-111F	McDonnell F-4C Phantom II	McDonnell F-4D Phantom II	McDonnell F-4E Phantom II	Northrop F-5A Freedom Fighter
First Flight*	1964	1963	1967	1967	1963
Wing span	63' (spread) 32' (swept)	38'5"	38'5"	38'5"	25'10"
Length	73'6"	58'3"	58'3"	63'	47'2"
Gross weight	95,333 lb	51,441 lb	51,577 lb	53,848 lb	13,433 lb
Top speed	Mach 1.5	Mach 1.5	Mach 1.5	Mach 1.5	Mach 1.5
Range	3378 mi	1926 mi	1844 mi	1885 mi	1318 mi
Engine	Pratt & Whitney JF30 turbofan (2)	General Electric J79 turbojet (2)	General Electric J79 turbojet (2)	General Electric J79 turbojet (2)	General Electric J79 turbojet (2)
Engine thrust	25,100 lb	17,000 lb	17,000 lb	17,900 lb	4080 lb

* First flights are for series prototypes, other data is for variants listed except Phantom II types.

systems were merged and new designations were assigned to existing aircraft. The Navy's F4H-1s and F4H-2s became F-4A and F-4B, while the F-110 became F-4C.

Deliveries of F-4Cs and reconnaissance RF-4Cs to the Tactical Air Command began in 1964. The subsequent improved F-4D series first flew in 1965, with deliveries in 1966. Navy F-4Bs and Air Force F-4Cs were committed to combat over Vietnam in 1964 and 1965, respectively. Air Force Phantoms emerged victorious from their first encounters with MiG-17s on 10 July 1965, but no further aerial combat occurred until 1966. The Phantom had been designed to function without guns and relied entirely on air-to-air missiles under the theory that guns were old-fashioned and superfluous to modern air warfare. In real combat, however, pilots quickly discovered the fallacy of this theory, so a 20mm centerline gun pod was fitted to the bottom of the F-4Cs and F-4Ds. So important were guns that in postwar analyses of air-to-air combat it was shown that they were by far the most effective means of shooting down enemy aircraft.

To help address this shortcoming, McDonnell developed the F-4E, the first Phantom with an internally mounted gun. It first flew in 1967, but various teething troubles delayed its entry into Southeast Asia until 1969. Because of the self-imposed restrictions on American military aircraft, air-to-air combat was very limited until 1972. During that year, however, the air war intensified to an unprecedented level, with F-4Ds and F-4Es tangling with MiGs on a regular basis. Indeed, most of the victories scored by American pilots occurred in 1972, and all three of the Air Force pilots to make ace achieved this distinction during this year. In the final tally, the Phantom was credited with 107.5 of the 137 victories scored by the US Air Force in the war.

Above right: **In this closeup we see the victory stars on an F-4 Phantom II of the 388th Tactical Fighter Wing which shot down MiG 19s in September and October of 1972.** *Opposite:* **Overflying the picturesque European countryside—an F-4G Phantom II 'Wild Weasel' of the 81st Tactical Fighter Squadron, based at Spangdahlem AB, West Germany.** *Below opposite:* **'MiGbane' of the Vietnam War: Members of a flight of shark-faced F-4Es of the 488th Tactical Fighter Wing line up behind a Strategic Air Command KC-135 aerial refueling tanker. These F-4Es were preparing for a MiG CAP (MiG Combat Air Patrol). The 388th was organized in 1966, and had shot down 17 MiGs by its deactivation at the end of 1972. This included an enforced four-year hiatus in aerial combat from 1968 to 1972, instituted when President Lyndon Johnson restricted all aerial strikes and combat operations to areas below the 19th parallel. The McDonnell F-4 Phantom II scored the vast majority of American victories over MiGs in Vietnam.**

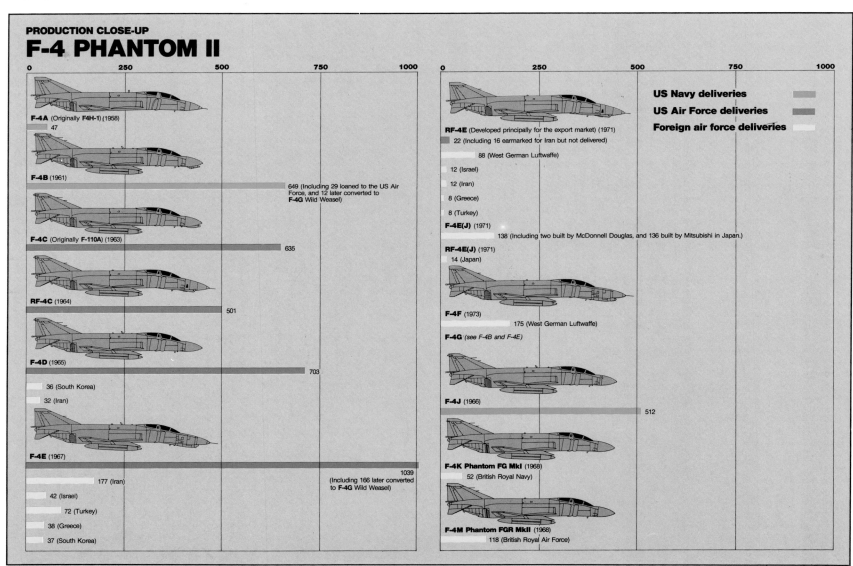

PRODUCTION CLOSE-UP
F-4 PHANTOM II

US Navy deliveries
US Air Force deliveries
Foreign air force deliveries

F-4A (Originally F4H-1) (1958)
47

F-4B (1961)
649 (Including 29 loaned to the US Air Force, and 12 later converted to **F-4G** Wild Weasel)

F-4C (Originally F-110A) (1963)
635

RF-4C (1964)
501

F-4D (1965)
703
36 (South Korea)
32 (Iran)

F-4E (1967)
1039 (Including 166 later converted to **F-4G** Wild Weasel)
177 (Iran)
42 (Israel)
72 (Turkey)
38 (Greece)
37 (South Korea)

RF-4E (Developed principally for the export market) (1971)
22 (Including 16 earmarked for Iran but not delivered)
88 (West German Luftwaffe)
12 (Israel)
12 (Iran)
8 (Greece)
8 (Turkey)

F-4E(J) (1971)
138 (Including two built by McDonnell Douglas, and 136 built by Mitsubishi in Japan.)

RF-4E(J) (1971)
14 (Japan)

F-4F (1973)
175 (West German Luftwaffe)

F-4G (see F-4B and F-4E)

F-4J (1966)
512

F-4K Phantom FG MkI (1968)
52 (British Royal Navy)

F-4M Phantom FGR MkII (1968)
118 (British Royal Air Force)

POSTWAR US AIR FORCE NON-COMBAT AIRCRAFT

Postwar US Air Force Transports

Specifications*	Boeing C-97G Stratofreighter	Fairchild C-119G Flying Boxcar	Douglas C-124C Globemaster II	Douglas C-133B Cargomaster	Boeing KC-135A Stratotanker
First Flight	1944	1950	1950	1956	1954**
Wing span	141'3"	109'4"	174'2"	179'8"	130'10"
Length	117'5"	86'6"	130'5"	157'3"	136'3"
Gross weight	175,000 lb	85,000 lb	195,500 lb	275,000 lb	297,000 lb
Cruising speed	300 mph	200 mph	304 mph	359 mph	600 mph
Range	4300 mi	1770 mi	1200 mi	3975 mi	5000 mi
Engine	Pratt & Whitney R4360 (4)	Wright R3350 cyclones (2)	Pratt & Whitney R4360 (4)	Pratt & Whitney T34 turboprop (4)	Pratt & Whitney J57 turbojet (4)
Engine rating	3500 hp	3500 hp	3800 hp	6500 hp	13,750 lb thrust

* First flights are for series prototypes, other data is for variants listed.
** The KC-135 tanker and C-135 transports (Boeing Model 717) are both derived from the 367-80 jetliner prototype as is the Model 707 jetliner.

At left: A USAF C-124 Globemaster overflies San Francisco Bay, with 1950s San Francisco at background left and the Oakland Bay Bridge at background right. The C-124 had a maximum payload of 68,500 pounds or 200 passengers, and dwarfed earlier transports. The even bigger Douglas C-133 Cargomaster *(above)* was typical of a transport model which could haul 80,000 pounds of cargo. One of the most recognized appellations in military air transport history is that of the Fairchild C-119 Flying Boxcar; *below,* in a scene that was typical for the Korean War, a USAF Far East Air Forces C-119 flies over the rugged Korean landscape, once again delivering the goods to US troops.

Above left: A Boeing KC-135 refuels a Boeing B-52. The KC-135 Stratotanker has a cargo fuel capacity of 31,200 US gallons. *Above:* A Stratotanker, with boom 'off duty,' flies past Mt Rainier. C-135 variants include transport aircraft—C-135As, Bs and VC-135s. Also there are WC-135B weather reconnaissance craft, EC-135 (A, B, J, K and L) electronic reconnaissance and flying command post aircraft, as well as RC-135A and B reconnaissance and photo-reconnaissance aircraft. Conversions of these versatile planes occur often, and there is a large shadow area of types, including C-135-derivative high-tech test beds. *Below:* The Boeing C-97 Stratofreighter, a variant of the Strato cruiser airliner.

Postwar Military Training Aircraft

Specifications[*]	Lockheed T-33A T-Bird	North American T-28A Trojan	North American T-2A Buckeye	Cessna T-37B Tweety Bird	Northrop T-38A Talon
First Flight	1949	1949	1958	1958	1959
Wing span	38'11"	40'1"	35'10"	33'9"	25'3"
Length	37'9"	32'	38'7"	29'3"	46'5"
Gross weight	15,100 lb	6365 lb	10,000 lb	6600 lb	12,093 lb
Cruising speed	543 mph	250 mph	400 mph	360 mph	812 mph
Range	1200 mi	1000 mi	963 mi	870 mi	1093 mi
Engine	Allison J33 Turbojet (1)	Wright R1300 Cyclone (1)	Westinghouse J34 Turbojet (1)	Continental J69 Turbojet (2)	General Electric J85 Turbojet (2)
Engine rating	4600 lb thrust	800 hp	3400 lb thrust	1025 lb thrust	2680 lb thrust

[*] First flights are for series prototype, other data is for variant named.

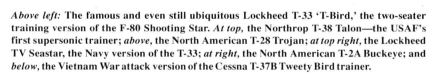

Above left: The famous and even still ubiquitous Lockheed T-33 'T-Bird,' the two-seater training version of the F-80 Shooting Star. *At top,* the Northrop T-38 Talon—the USAF's first supersonic trainer; *above,* the North American T-28 Trojan; *at top right,* the Lockheed TV Seastar, the Navy version of the T-33; *at right,* the North American T-2A Buckeye; and *below,* the Vietnam War attack version of the Cessna T-37B Tweety Bird trainer.

Postwar Military Research Aircraft

Specifications	Bell X-1	Douglas D-558-2* Skyrocket	Douglas X-3 Stilletto	Bell X-5**	North American X-15
First Flight	1946	1948	1952	1951	1959
Wing span	28'	25'	22'8"	32'9"	22'
Length	31'	45'3"	66'9"	32'4"	50'
Gross weight	13,400 lb	15,226 lb	22,400 lb	10,000 lb	31,276 lb
Top speed	1000 mph	1327 mph	706 mph	705 mph	4532 mph
Research Goal	Achieve Mach 1 speeds	Achieve Mach 2 speeds	Sustained flight at supersonic speeds	Variable geometry wings	Ultra high speed and altitude tests
Engine	Reaction Motors 6000 rocket engine (1)	Reaction Motors XLR-8-RM-5 rocket engine (1)	Westinghouse XJ 34 Turbojet (2)	Allison J35 Turbojet (1)	Thiokol (Reaction Motors) XLR99-RM-2 rocket engine (1)
Engine thrust	6000 lb thrust	11,000 lb thrust	4200 lb thrust	4900 lb thrust	70,000 lb thrust

* The dissimilar D-558-1 Skystreak first flew in 1947.   ** Based on the German Messerschmitt P.1101 of 1944 which never flew.

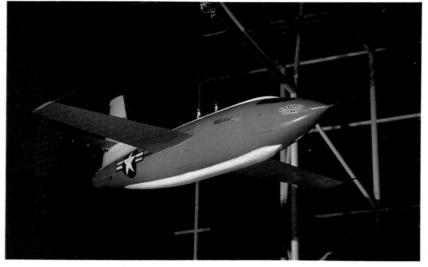

Captain Chuck Yeager became the first man to break the sound barrier when he piloted the Bell X-1 *at right*, named (for his wife) *Glamorous Glennis*, to a speed of 967 mph at 70,140 feet on 14 October 1947. The X-1's air-launch 'mother ship' was a B-29.

The North American X-15 was an air-launched manned rocket plane that flew into the edge of space, earning several of its pilots astronaut wings. The highest X-15 flight was to a record 354,200 feet on 22 August 1963. There were three X-15s, and X-15 Number Two was upgraded to become the even higher performance X-15-A2—seen *above*, with external propellant tanks that would be jettisoned at Mach 2. *Below* is the X-15-A2 with a coating of reapplicable heat-ablative material; however, on the 3 October 1967 flight, high-speed heat damage to the X-15-A2 forced its retirement. The three X-15 aircraft made 199 flights from 8 June 1959 to 24 October 1968, with just one fatal accident (on flight 191).

Above left, clockwise from bottom center: The Douglas X-3 Stiletto, a jet powered experimental aircraft designed for, but unable to attain, sustained flight at extremely high speeds; the Bell X-1A, a supersonic rocket powered successor to the X-1, which reached speeds in excess of 1600 mph; the Navy's jet-powered D-558 Skystreak (which was aka the 'Crimson Test Tube'); the Convair XF-92, built to test the delta-wing configuration later used on the F-102 and the F-106; the Bell X-5 variable-wing aircraft, built to investigate the effects of changing the wings' rate of sweep while in flight; the Navy's rocket-powered Douglas D-558-2 Skyrocket, a successor to the Skystreak, which set an altitude record for piloted aircraft at 79,494 feet; and the twin-jet Northrop X-4, built to explore the flight characteristics of the swept-back, all-wing configuration at trans sonic speeds.

POSTWAR COMMERCIAL AIRCRAFT

When the Second World War ended, the future of commercial aviation looked very promising. Naturally, aircraft builders assumed that they would automatically be included in the postwar boom. They were wrong.

The 'airplane in every garage' prediction that had been made simply didn't come true. A great many builders lost money on 'personal' airplane schemes. In the case of the airlines, traffic did increase dramatically, but a great deal of that growth was among smaller carriers who could buy surplus C-47s and turn them back into DC-3s. There was a market for large aircraft but competition would be fierce.

All of the major aircraft builders plunged in immediately. Both Douglas and Lockheed lost money on abortive small aircraft, but they went straight to the top of the heap on the large four-engined aircraft that the big airlines wanted. Douglas quickly revived its prewar DC-4 program (which had been drafted into the USAAF as the C-54), while Lockheed got its Constellation back on its original commercial track. Boeing entered the field with a civilian version of its USAAF C-97, (see pp 144–147), which was called Stratocruiser. Both Martin and Convair entered the market with twin-engined aircraft, but they suffered from competition presented by cheap war surplus transports.

The DC-4 also suffered from competition with surplus C-54s, but Douglas was able to address this problem by bringing out a much improved—though similar appearing—aircraft designated DC-6. Both American Airlines and United Air Lines started integrating them into their fleets in 1947. The DC-6 was soon followed by the larger DC-7, which first went into service in 1953 with United Air Lines. The initial DC-7 and DC-7B types were followed by the very long range DC-7C. The '7Cs' carried the nickname 'Seven Seas,' which served as a clever indication of their range. The DC-7C made its operational debut in 1956 on Pan American's vast Pacific route network.

At left: King of postwar airliner builders, Donald Wills Douglas strikes a friendly pose with a Douglas DC-4 airliner. *Below left,* front to back: Why Douglas dominated postwar commercial airline flight—the Douglas DC-7, DC-6, DC-4 and DC-3S, or Super DC-3.

Above: The DC-7C 'Seven Seas' (shown here in Belgian World Airlines livery) had the range to fly almost anywhere in the world, could carry almost four times the passenger load of a DC-3 and 30 percent more than a DC-4. *Below:* An American Airlines Douglas DC-6.

The Lockheed Constellation—'Connie' to her friends—was originally ordered by Howard Hughes' Trans World Airlines (TWA) in 1939. However, before the first Connie could be built, she was diverted to the USAAF as the XC-69. The XC-69 first flew on 9 January 1943, and 22 Constellations on order from TWA and Pan Am were built and diverted to the USAAF over the next two years.

TWA took delivery of its first commercial Model 49 Constellation on 1 October 1945, less than one month after the war ended, and went on to become one of the major users of the big plane. Because of the Connie's long range and reliability, she became popular with the major airlines of the world on their long distance transoceanic routes. In addition to TWA and Pan American, Constellations (principally Model 749) were also ordered by American Overseas, British Overseas, Air France, Eastern, Lufthansa, South African, Belgium's Sabena, Air India and the Netherlands' KLM. In 1952, Lockheed introduced a new and larger Model 1049 *Super* Constellation, which was in turn followed by the Model 1649 Starliner in 1956. Both were great improvements over the earlier Constellations, but they now faced serious competition from jetliners.

Boeing's Model 377 Stratocruiser was a solid aircraft with an exceptional reputation, whose only fault was that it was seriously outsold by the Douglas and Lockheed four-engined liners. Having first flown in July 1947, the big plane went into service with Pan Am and Northwest on their long range overseas routes.

When the box score on sales of postwar American four-engined airliners was tallied, Douglas clearly retained its place as the world leader in airliner development that it had earned with the DC-3. Taking into account commercial aircraft and excluding military derivatives, there were 600 DC-6s, 338 DC-7s, 78 DC-4s, 494 Lockheed Constellations and 56 Boeing Stratocruisers. These American totals exceeded the rest of the world combined.

At top: **A Pan American Clipper Service Lockheed Model 649 Constellation.** *At right:* **A Trans World Airlines Model 1049 Super Constellation winging over early-1950s Manhattan.** *Above:* **Service in the plush 'Sky Lounge' aboard a Lockheed Super 'Connie.'**

Squeezed between the surplus-dominated market of the late 1940s and the jetliner-dominated market of the 1960s, the big four-engined airliners carved an important niche in aviation history in a brief span of time. However, they will be remembered most by the people who flew in them for the unparalleled luxury they offered. The accommodations they offered were simply not possible in the cramped liners of the 1930s and are only a dream aboard the much larger but equally cramped jetliners of today.

The notion of building jetliners came immediately after the war amid the rush to build military jets. Commercial aircraft were, however, a bit more complex because of the need to offer both performance *and* economy.

The world's first commercial jetliner type was the British DeHavilland Comet that went into service in 1952. However, it was plagued by a series of crashes and had to be grounded. In the United States, the planemakers watched from the sidelines. Douglas, Lockheed and Boeing were all studying jetliners, but the Comet debacle brought their practicality into serious question. Both Douglas and Lockheed, as we've noted, had successful propliner programs in place, so they were wary about a jump into jetliners. Because Boeing's Stratocruiser was lagging in the propliner market, almost anything they might do was better than doing nothing. Furthermore, with its B-47 and B-52 military aircraft, Boeing had developed an unexcelled expertise in large jets, which would now prove invaluable.

Above: One of the many postwar uses of the Constellation was as the US Air Force RC-121D Aircraft Early Warning flying radar station. An interesting footnote to the history of the versatile Connie is that US President Dwight D Eisenhower's Air Force One was a Constellation. *At right and below:* The Model 377 Stratocruiser was the last Boeing product to offer Pullman-style sleeping berths. The Stratocruiser was a great plane, but lost out in the marketplace to the more popular Douglas and Lockheed airliners.

Postwar Four-engined Propeller-driven Airliners

Specifications	Lockheed 49 Constellation	Douglas DC-6	Boeing 377 Stratocruiser	Lockheed 1049 Super Constellation	Douglas DC-7
First Flight	1945*	1946	1947**	1950	1953
Wing span	123'	117'6"	141'3"	123'	117'6"
Length	95'3"	100'7"	110'4"	113'9"	108'11"
Gross weight	90,000 lb	107,000 lb	145,000 lb	120,000 lb	144,000 lb
Cruising speed	300 mph	308 mph	300 mph	331 mph	334 mph
Range	2300 mi	2990 mi	4600 mi	4820 mi	5635 mi
Engine	Wright R3350 Cyclones	Pratt & Whitney R2800	Pratt & Whitney Wasp Majors	Wright R3350 Cyclones	Wright R3350 Cyclones
Engine rating	2200 hp	2400 hp	3500 hp	2700 hp	3250 hp

* The prototype flew in USAAF markings as C-69 in 1943, but the commercial aircraft were first flown in 1945.
** The Model 377 was essentially a commercial version of the USAAF C-97 (Model 367) in 1944.

For reasons of secrecy, the Boeing jetliner program was given the same Model number (367) as the old propeller-driven C-97 transport, which had preceded the Model 377 Stratocruiser. It was not until after the prototype made its first flight on 15 July 1954 that the famous Model number '707' was unveiled. Both Pan American and American Airlines placed orders for the Boeing 707 and the US Air Force ordered the nearly identical Model 717 for use as a transport and aerial refueling tanker. The first Model 717 was delivered to the Air Force in July 1956 under the military designation C-135, although most of the Air Force versions would be delivered as tankers, designated and named KC-135 Stratotanker.

Pan American received its first 707 on 15 August 1958, three months ahead of schedule, and Continental, Braniff, Air France and Qantas followed shortly. Pan Am began service on 26 October 1958 over the transatlantic routes and it soon revolutionized air travel in that market by slashing travel time. Subsequent 707 derivatives included the intermediate range 707-220 (Model 720), which first flew with United Air Lines in 1960, and the extra long range 707-320 'Intercontinental,' which first flew with Pan American in 1959.

Boeing had been aced in the propeller airliner market only to come roaring back with a full house in the form of their jet-engine 707 *(below and right)*, the plane that rang in the age of the commercial jet airliner. *Above:* The 367-80, the prototype for the 707 series.

While Boeing took an early lead in the jetliner market, Douglas moved quickly with a four-engined jetliner of its own. The Douglas DC-8 made its first flight in 1958, four years behind the Boeing 707, and entered service in August 1958 with United Air Lines. Boeing had seized the lead, and while Douglas would never catch up, the DC-8 was a successful plane and it helped close the gap. Lockheed, meanwhile, had decided to sit out the first round of jetliner development.

While the 707 and DC-8 were dividing the worldwide market for longer range jetliners, Boeing had diagnosed a substantial market for a medium range jetliner that would be as economical on short to medium distances as the 707 was on transcontinental and transoceanic routes. The result was the Boeing 727 trijet, which first flew on 9 February 1963. Entering service with United Air Lines in December of the same year, the 727 remained in production until 1984 and became the biggest selling jetliner in history. If you take into account that most DC-3s in the world were actually military C-47s that were sold into the commercial market second-hand, then the 727 ranks as the biggest selling *airliner* in history!

continued on page 164

Below: **United Air Lines' first Douglas DC-8s arrive for passenger carriage in 1958, four years after the initial deployment of Boeing's 707s.** *At right:* **The first flight of the DC-8, on 30 May 1958.** *Below opposite:* **Two examples of the Boeing 727-200, a longer and upgraded version of Boeing's second jetliner triumph, the variable-range trijet 727.** *Opposite:* **A Trans Australia Airlines Boeing 727 shows a well-known profile.**

Above: The Boeing 727 is easily the most well-known airliner in service today, and its familiar shape has been part of the landscape at airports all over the world for years. *Below left:* The flight deck of a 727. The 727-100 *(below)* and the longer 727-200 are so good that the 727 series is the largest selling airliner in history. The airplane was, from its first service flight, virtually trouble-free and extremely reliable. As they become long of tooth, however, they will be replaced on many airlines with newer designs.

continued from page 160

As the ubiquitous 727 was starting to make its mark with the world's airlines, Boeing was beginning to contemplate building a 'family' of jetliners. The 707 and 727 were the 'large' and 'medium' jetliners, but there was still room for a 'small.' The world's fleet of small propeller-driven airliners was gradually aging to the point where planes needed to be replaced and replacement types were no longer in production. Boeing offered a solution in the form of its diminutive 737, which entered service with Eastern Air Lines on 1 February 1967.

Meanwhile, thoughts of a jetliner 'family' concept were not lost on Douglas. Boeing had revolutionized the airline industry with the 707 and 727, while Douglas played catch-up with the DC-8. However, Douglas began looking at the *short* range market even *before* Boeing began work on the 737. The result was the most successful Douglas airliner since the DC-3. Designated DC-9, it made its first flight on 25 February 1965, two years after the 727, and went into service with Delta Airlines in December of the same year. It was high-tailed (like Boeing's 727), twin-jet (like Boeing's yet unborn 737), and it offered customers a wide range of choices in size. For example, the DC-9 series 10 (1965) was 104 feet long, the series 30 (1966) was 119 feet long, the series 40 (1967) was 125.5 feet long and the series 50 (1974) was 133 feet long.

The most successful Douglas airliner since the DC-3, the DC-9 made its first flight on 25 February 1965. The DC-9 Series 30 craft shown *above* was one of several models of the DC-9 series (see text, this page). *At right:* A Douglas DC-9 Series 40 participates in greeting the *Queen Mary* as that famous luxury liner steams toward its final berth at Long Beach, California on 8 December 1967. *Below:* Boeing's short-distance contender, the 737.

First Generation Jetliners

Specifications[*]	Boeing 707	Douglas DC-8	Boeing 727	Douglas DC-9	Boeing 737
First Flight[*]	1954	1958	1963	1965	1967
Wing span	142'5"	142'5"	89'4"	93'	93'
Length	152'11"	150'6"	153'2"	104'4"	100'
Gross weight	316,000 lb	355,000 lb	208,000 lb	90,700 lb	116,000 lb
Cruising speed	600 mph	570 mph	600 mph	550 mph	575 mph
Range	4200 mi	4773 mi	2800 mi	1565 mi	2000 mi
Engine	Pratt & Whitney JT4A Turbojets(4)	Pratt & Whitney JT3C Turbofans(3)	Pratt & Whitney JT8D Turbo(4)	Pratt & Whitney JT8D Turbofans(2)	Pratt & Whitney JT8D Turbofans(2)
Engine thrust	15,800 lb	19,000 lb	16,000 lb	12,250 lb	16,000 lb

[*] First flight dates are for series prototypes, data is for 707-320, DC-8-10, 727-200, DC-9-10 and 737-300.
The Douglas planes *were* the first of their series.

The DC-9 series 80, which was first flown in 1979, was both the longest and most successful. At 147 feet 10 inches, it was less than five feet shorter than the 727 series 200. In 1983, McDonnell Douglas Corporation (the parent company of Douglas Aircraft since 1967) decided to market subsequent DC-9-80s as all-new airplanes to reflect the new systems that had been incorporated into the aircraft since the design of the original DC-9 nearly two decades before. To underscore the McDonnell Douglas identity, the DC-9-80 was now redesignated as MD-80 and is discussed in the subsequent chapter *American Jetliners Today*.

The largest airliner ever built found its way into Boeing's 'family' of jetliners by way of a 1964 US Air Force requirement for an enormous jet airlifter that could carry double the payload of any other transport in existence. Ultimately, Lockheed beat both Boeing and Douglas in the competition for the huge airplane that would be designated C-5.

Boeing, however, decided to use what it had learned in producing the C-5 proposal in a commercial aircraft. By early 1966 Boeing had a design on paper which won it a $525 million contract from Pan American, and a program was launched. On 9 February 1969 the Boeing 747 took to the air. It was the largest jetliner in the world—and probably the largest that the world will see in this century. The prototype handled like an airplane one-fifth its size and received rave reviews from every test pilot who took the controls. On 22 January 1970, Pan Am inaugurated service with the 747 on its transatlantic route. Despite the oil crisis in the early 1970s, the huge jet was soon standard equipment for every American airline that flew high density transcontinental or transoceanic routes, as well as for every other major national flag carrier.

In addition to the basic 747-100 and 747-200 passenger planes, Boeing developed a 747-200F freighter, as well as a 747-200C 'convertible' that could be used for either freight *or* passengers. The 747SP (Special Performance), a shortened version introduced in May 1975, had the longest range of any production aircraft in the commercial market. In December 1976, for example, Pan Am put the 747SP into service nonstop on its 7200 mile San Francisco to Sydney run. Another 747SP flew 10,290 miles nonstop from Seattle to Capetown on a delivery flight.

In the late 1960s, at the same time that Boeing was plunging forward on its 747 project, both Lockheed and Douglas (a component of McDonnell

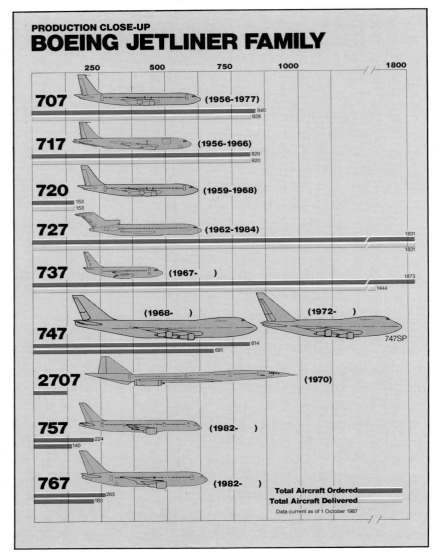

PRODUCTION CLOSE-UP
BOEING JETLINER FAMILY

	250	500	750	1000	1800
707			(1956-1977) 845 / 828		
717			(1956-1966) 820 / 820		
720	153 / 153		(1959-1968)		
727			(1962-1984)		1831 / 1831
737			(1967-)		1873 / 1444
747		681 / 814 (1968-)		(1972-) 747SP	
2707			(1970)		
757	140 / 224		(1982-)		
767	263 / 183		(1982-)		

Total Aircraft Ordered
Total Aircraft Delivered
Data current as of 1 October 1987

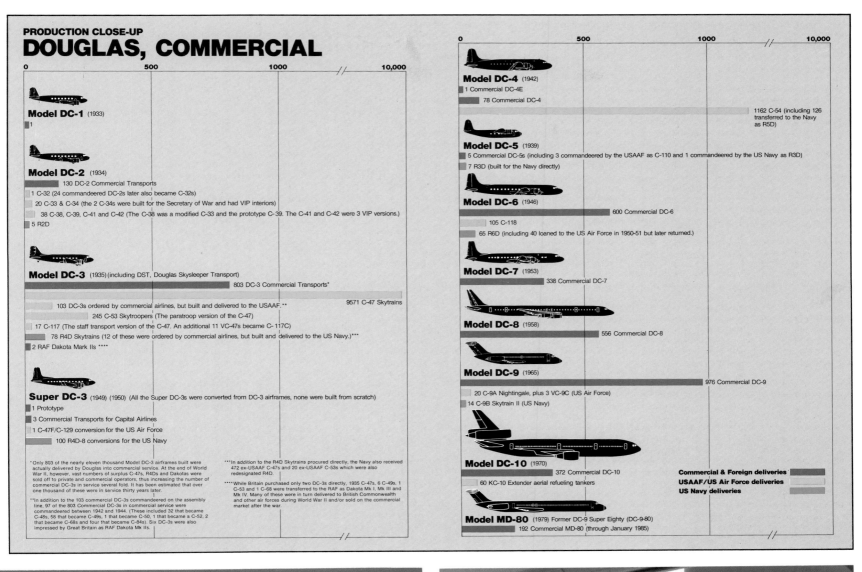

PRODUCTION CLOSE-UP
DOUGLAS, COMMERCIAL

Model DC-1 (1933)
1

Model DC-2 (1934)
130 DC-2 Commercial Transports
1 C-32 (24 commandeered DC-2s later also became C-32s)
20 C-33 & C-34 (the 2 C-34s were built for the Secretary of War and had VIP interiors)
38 C-38, C-39, C-41 and C-42 (The C-38 was a modified C-33 and the prototype C-39. The C-41 and C-42 were 3 VIP versions.)
5 R2D

Model DC-3 (1935) (including DST, Douglas Skysleeper Transport)
803 DC-3 Commercial Transports*
103 DC-3s ordered by commercial airlines, but built and delivered to the USAAF.**
9571 C-47 Skytrains
245 C-53 Skytroopers (The paratroop version of the C-47)
17 C-117 (The staff transport version of the C-47. An additional 11 VC-47s became C-117C)
78 R4D Skytrains (12 of these were ordered by commercial airlines, but built and delivered to the US Navy.)***
2 RAF Dakota Mark IIs ****

Super DC-3 (1949) (1950) (All the Super DC-3s were converted from DC-3 airframes, none were built from scratch)
1 Prototype
3 Commercial Transports for Capital Airlines
1 C-47F/C-129 conversion for the US Air Force
100 R4D-8 conversions for the US Navy

* Only 803 of the nearly eleven thousand Model DC-3 airframes built were actually delivered by Douglas into commercial service. At the end of World War II, however, vast numbers of surplus C-47s, R4Ds and Dakotas were sold off to private and commercial operators, thus increasing the number of commercial DC-3s in service several fold. It has been estimated that over one thousand of these were in service thirty years later.

** In addition to the 103 commercial DC-3s commandeered on the assembly line, 97 of the 803 Commercial DC-3s in commercial service were commandeered between 1942 and 1944. (These included 32 that became C-48s, 58 that became C-49s, 1 that became C-50, 1 that became a C-52, 2 that became C-68s and four that became C-84s. Six DC-3s were also impressed by Great Britain as RAF Dakota Mk IIs.

*** In addition to the R4D Skytrains procured directly, the Navy also received 472 ex-USAAF C-47s and 20 ex-USAAF C-53s which were also redesignated R4D.

**** While Britain purchased only two DC-3s directly, 1935 C-47s, 6 C-49s, 1 C-53 and 1 C-68 were transferred to the RAF as Dakota Mk I, Mk III and Mk IV. Many of these were in turn delivered to British Commonwealth and other air forces during World War II and/or sold on the commercial market after the war.

Model DC-4 (1942)
1 Commercial DC-4E
78 Commercial DC-4
1162 C-54 (including 126 transferred to the Navy as R5D)

Model DC-5 (1939)
5 Commercial DC-5s (including 3 commandeered by the USAAF as C-110 and 1 commandeered by the US Navy as R3D)
7 R3D (built for the Navy directly)

Model DC-6 (1946)
600 Commercial DC-6
105 C-118
65 R6D (including 40 loaned to the US Air Force in 1950-51 but later returned.)

Model DC-7 (1953)
338 Commercial DC-7

Model DC-8 (1958)
556 Commercial DC-8

Model DC-9 (1965)
976 Commercial DC-9
20 C-9A Nightingale, plus 3 VC-9C (US Air Force)
14 C-9B Skytrain II (US Navy)

Model DC-10 (1970)
372 Commercial DC-10
60 KC-10 Extender aerial refueling tankers

Commercial & Foreign deliveries
USAAF/US Air Force deliveries
US Navy deliveries

Model MD-80 (1979) Former DC-9 Super Eighty (DC-9-80)
192 Commercial MD-80 (through January 1985)

At left: **The Boeing 747 is the largest airliner in the world.** *Above:* **Inside, at the base of the staircase leading to the 747's upper deck.**

Douglas as of 1967) were also contemplating 'jumbo jets.' It was generally known in the industry that there was a market for a jetliner whose passenger capacity was between that of the Boeing 707 and DC-8 (250 plus, depending on seating arrangement) on one side and the huge 747 (about 500, depending on seating) on the other. Both Lockheed and Douglas proceeded with plans to fill this gap, despite uncertainty over whether there would be room in this gap for *two* jetliners.

By early 1968, the two planes had taken form on paper and the companies were ready to start taking orders. Lockheed's entry, and the company's first jetliner, was the L-1011 TriStar, a 400 passenger double-aisled jumbo jet with two wing-mounted high-bypass turbofan engines on the wings and a third in the tail. The Douglas entry was the DC-10, and it was *also* a 400 passenger double-aisled jumbo jet with two wing-mounted high-bypass turbofan engines on the wings and a third in the tail. The only immediately discernible difference was that the L-1011's tail-mounted engine had an 'S-duct' connecting it to the intake, while the DC-10's was of a simpler 'straight-through' design. *(See diagrams below.)*

During the spring of 1968 the five largest airlines in the United States lined up to buy the 400 passenger jetliner that market research, and conventional wisdom, said they needed. Had a single aircraft been available, its builder would have made a killing. However, there was not one but *two,* so they split the market. The nation's two largest airlines—American and United—bought the DC-10, while the next three—Eastern, Delta and TWA—bought the L-1011.

The DC-10 made its first flight on 29 August 1970, followed by the L-1011 on 17 November 1970. Both airplanes served their customers well, but there were serious problems with each. For starters, the development costs had seriously strapped both companies. Then the bankruptcy of Rolls Royce (the TriStar engine supplier) helped to push Lockheed to the brink of bankruptcy, and a couple of serious DC-10 crashes severely eroded public confidence in that airplane.

Ultimately, the market for the two aircraft grew to include most of the world's major flag carriers. Although it was a split market, Lockheed built 250 L-1011s before it closed the assembly line in 1985, while McDonnell Douglas built 367 DC-10s through 1983. In addition to these, 60 DC-10s were ordered by the US Air Force as refueling tankers under the designation KC-10, and in 1984 the DC-10 commercial assembly line was reopened with an order for five brand new aircraft from Federal Express. Since that time McDonnell Douglas has been actively marketing a much improved DC-10 concept, which will carry the designation MD-11, when and if it goes into production.

Smaller than the 747, but 'Jumbo Jets' nonetheless. *Above:* A quintet of Douglas DC-10 airliners. This trijet, 400-passenger design bore a striking similarity to the Lockheed L-1011 design, and in fact the two airliners were in direct competition. *At right:* A picturesque view of a Lockheed L-1011 TriStar in flight.

Douglas DC-10

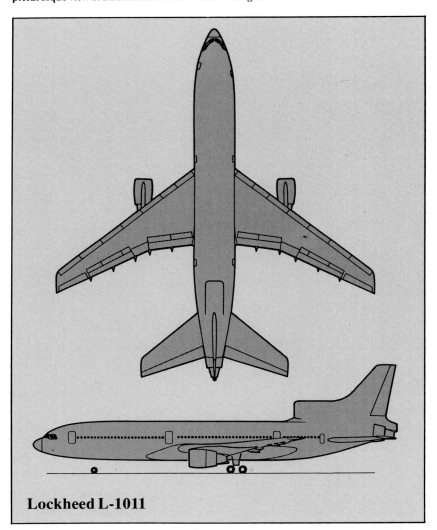

Lockheed L-1011

The Widebody Jumbo Jets

Specifications	Boeing 747	Douglas[*] DC-10	Lockheed L-1011	Boeing 747SP
First Flight	1969	1970	1970	1975
Wing span	195'8"	155'4"	155'4"	195'8"
Length	231'10"	182'3"	177'8"	184'9"
Gross weight	710-833,000 lb	444,000 lb	430,000 lb	690,000 lb
Cruising speed	600 mph	587 mph	600 mph	600 mph
Range	6563 mi	6325 mi	5500 mi	6900 mi
Engine	(Four turbofans) customer choice of: a. Pratt & Whitney JT9D b. General Electric CF-6 c. Rolls Royce RB211	(Three turbofans) General Electric CF-6	(Three turbofans) Rolls Royce RB211	(Four turbofans) customer choice of: a. Pratt & Whitney b. General Electric CF-6 c. Rolls Royce RB211
Engine thrust	a. 53,000 lb b. 52,500 lb c. 50,100 lb	40,000 lb	42,000 lb	a. 53,000 lb b. 52,500 lb c. 50,100 lb

[*] Douglas Aircraft merged with McDonnell Aircraft in 1967 to form McDonnell Douglas Corporation, but with the DC-10 was developed entirely by the Douglas component of the corporation.

Boeing 747 series

In addition to being the apex of contemporary passenger liners, the Boeing 747 is also great in other arenas of aviation. *At left,* left and right: Views of the Boeing 747 and 747SP. The 747SP (Special Performance) has the longest range of any aircraft in the commercial market, with a standard range of 6900 miles. Some 47 feet shorter than the regular-dimension 747s, the 747SP has been known to fly distances up to 10,290 miles.

For such a big plane, the 747 handles like a dream. It was originally designed in competition with the Lockheed C-5 as a military mega-transport. Boeing lost the C-5 competition, but went on to develop 747 transport models—the 747-200F Freighter and the 747-200C (convertible for either passengers or freight, or a combination of both). Several 747-200Fs fly the heaviest routine service takeoff weights in the world for Cargolux, an air freight line that operates out of Luxembourg, Belgium.

At right: A cutaway view of a 747-200C, showing passenger and cargo space, and the staircase (this one a spiral) which leads to the upper deck (see, also, photo on page 167). *Above:* A Northwest Orient Cargo 747 Freighter glides through the air with ease. Other applications include the National Aeronautics and Space Administration's use of a specially-modified 747 to haul their Space Shuttle orbiters.

Part Four

American Aircraft Today

MILITARY AIRCRAFT TODAY

The range of military aircraft in service today includes a variety of older, previously discussed planes such as the Boeing KC-135 Stratotanker and the McDonnell Douglas F-4 Phantom. The majority of the important combat aircraft in the US Air Force and the US Navy today form a generation that was developed in the 1970s which became fully operational in the 1980s. These include the Navy's Grumman F-14 Tomcat and McDonnell Douglas F/A-18 Hornet, and the Air Force's McDonnell Douglas F-15 Eagle and General Dynamics F-16 Fighting Falcon. The Air Force has also recently brought on line its first all-new strategic bomber in a quarter century: the Rockwell B-1.

As for military transport aircraft, the Air Force's Military Airlift Command has a three-plane family of airlifters, all built by Lockheed, that provides a well-rounded answer to most of its requirements. In the area of high performance reconnaissance, the Lockheed TR-1—successor to the infamous U-2—remains in production, while the Lockheed SR-71 Blackbird is still untouchable in terms of speed and altitude capability.

The Grumman F-14 Tomcat, the Navy's top air superiority fighter, is a worthy successor to the Grumman 'carrier-cat' tradition of World War II. It evolved in the late 1960s when the Navy withdrew from the TFX program which eventually begat the Air Force's F-111. Like the F-111, the Tomcat was designed with variable sweep wings. It made its first flight on 21 December 1970 and its first flight from a carrier deck in June 1972. In 1974, it became operational with VF-1 (*Wolf Pack*) and VF-2 (*Bounty Hunters*) on the USS *Enterprise* in the Pacific, and with VF-14 *(Tophatters)* and VF-32 (*Swordsmen*) on the USS *John F Kennedy* in the Mediterranean. Designed to carry the AIM-54 Phoenix air-to-air missile as well as other armament, the Tomcat is one of the most potent fighters in the world today. In the first aerial combat since the Vietnam War involving American fighters, two F-14s of VF-41 (*Black Aces*)

Above: **The Navy's hot carrier fighter, the Mach 2.3 Grumman F-14 Tomcat. Note that its six Phoenix missiles are mounted on pylons located on its massive wing roots, not on its variable-sweep wings.** *Below:* **Top view of F-14s, with wings swept back fully, over the USS** *John F Kennedy.* **At right: An F-14A of** *Jolly Roger* **Squadron VF-84 of the USS** *Nimitz.*

aboard the USS *Nimitz* engaged and destroyed two Libyan Su-22s over the Gulf of Sidra in August 1981. Tomcats were also active in support of US Air Force strikes against terrorist bases in Libya in April 1986.

The McDonnell Douglas F-15 Eagle is the latest in a long line of McDonnell high performance fighters that includes the legendary F-4 Phantom. The Eagle was conceived in the late 1960s as the successor to the Phantom as the leading Air Force air superiority fighter. It was designed to incorporate all the lessons learned from practical experience in Vietnam. Like the F-14, it was a very large twin-engined fighter with an excellent thrust to weight ratio. The Eagle first flew on 17 July 1972 and the first F-15 unit, the First Tactical Fighter Wing at Langley AFB, became fully operational in January 1976.

The initial type, the F-15A, was accompanied by a two-seat trainer version designated F-15B. In June 1979, an improved F-15C made its appearance together with the F-15D combat-capable trainer version. Though the Eagle has not been used in combat by the United States, it has had its baptism of fire with the air force of Israel in which it performed incredibly. In June 1982, Israeli F-15 pilots shot down more than 50 Soviet-built Syrian fighters over the Bakaa Valley without losing a single Eagle!

The newest Eagle variant is the F-15E, a special bomb-carrying interdictor strike aircraft that evolved out of a project undertaken by the McDonnell component of McDonnell Douglas in the late 1970s. McDonnell adapted the back seat of a two-seat combat-capable Eagle trainer to serve an offensive air-to-ground weapons operator, redesigned the plane to carry such weapons, and offered it to the Air Force as the 'Strike Eagle' fighter-bomber. By 1983 the Air Force Tactical Air Command was seriously looking for a fighter/fighter-bomber

as a replacement for its aging F-111 long range interdictors and the 'Strike Eagle' became the Dual Role Fighter Demonstrator (DRFD).

On 24 February 1984, Chief of Staff General Charles Gabriel announced that the Air Force had decided to procure $1.5 billion worth of DRFD 'Strike Eagles' under the designation F-15E. Though the F-15E would weigh 19 percent more, it would have more than 95 percent of its components in common with an F-15D. It would be capable of carrying a twelve-ton bomb load, but could convert to air-to-air ordnance and serve in an air superiority role.

On 11 December 1986, the first F-15E made its maiden flight at McDonnell's Lambert Field at St Louis, Missouri. The F-15E, the descendant of the 'Strike Eagle,' was powered by a pair of Pratt & Whitney F100-200 turbofans with digital electronic fuel controls and fitted with both Hughes APG-70 radar and a Martin Marietta Low-Altitude Navigation & Targeting Infrared for Night (LANTIRN) system.

By mid-1987, the US Air Force had 711 Eagles of all types in service, primarily with its Tactical Air Command, US Air Forces in Europe, Pacific Air Forces and Alaskan Air Command. These were in turn augmented by 49 in service with the Air National Guard. The units using F-15s include both Tactical Fighter Squadrons and Fighter Interceptor Squadrons. The latter includes the 48th FIS at Langley AFB, Virginia, which is equipped with antisatellite (ASAT) weapons. Ultimately, the US Air Force and the Air National Guard will receive a total of 1266 F-15s of all types, including 392 F-15Es.

The Mach 2.5 hottest of the hot. *Below:* **Two USAF Tactical Air Command McDonnell Douglas F-15 Eagles. Note the AIM-7 Sparrow AAMs under their fuselages and the AIM-9 Sidewinders on their wing pylons.** *At right:* **US Air Forces in Europe (USAFE) F-15s over the Netherlands.**

McDonnell Douglas F-15 Eagle

This 'ghost' view of an F-15 shows most of its vital parts. The pink areas are the fuel tanks and fuel lines necessary to feed the Eagle's two Pratt & Whitney F100-PW-100 afterburning turbofans (in brown) that are each responsible for 23,930 lbs of the thrust that gets this craft to its Mach 2.5 maximum speed. The head-up instrument display is visible in the cockpit, as are the General Electric M61 revolving cannon on the left of the fuselage and the AIM-7 Sparrow Air-to-Air Missiles on the right of same.

The General Dynamics F-16 Fighting Falcon was conceived as an inexpensive lightweight fighter that the US Air Force could buy to complement its acquisition of the F-15. The first YF-16 was flown in February 1974 and through the rest of the year it was evaluated against the Northrop YF-17. In January 1975, the Falcon was selected and went into production, while the YF-17 project evolved into the F/A-18. The F-16 was also selected by the air forces of Belgium, Denmark, the Netherlands and Norway, and co-production arrangements were initiated with SONACA/SABCA in Belgium and Fokker in the Netherlands.

The Falcon first became operational in January 1979 with the 388th Tactical Fighter Wing at Hill AFB, Utah. Later in the year the air forces of Belgium and the Netherlands took delivery of their first domestically produced F-16s. Israel also became a customer for F-16s and in June 1981 used them to destroy the Osirak nuclear reactor facility near Baghdad, Iraq that was reportedly producing material for nuclear bombs.

The US Air Force also designated most of its Falcons as fighter-bombers, but in 1986, the Air Force found itself with a need for a lightweight air defense fighter to augment its heavier and more expensive F-15s, as well as its F-106 fleet, the latter of which was in its third decade of service. The choices were the Northrop F-20 Tigershark, a follow-on to the F-5 Tiger, and a variant of the F-16. The former was not in service with any air service anywhere in the world and, although it had received rave reviews from test pilots (including Chuck Yeager), it existed only in the form of a company-owned demonstrator.

In November 1986, the Air Force announced that it would take 270 F-16As, as they were replaced by F-16Cs, and retrofit them as air defense fighters. This retrofit would be the major part of an upgrade of 425 F-16As and F-16Bs that would take place at the Ogden Air Logistics Center at Hill AFB, Utah. The F-16A interceptors would roll out of the Ogden Center with provision for Westinghouse AN/APG-66 radar and able to participate in the Rockwell Navstar Global Positioning System (GPS). Offensive hardware would include the AIM-7 Sparrow and AIM-120 AMRAAM air-to-air missiles, as well as the AIM-9s currently used on F-16s.

By April 1987, as work was progressing on the F-16A interceptor conversion at General Dynamics in Fort Worth, Texas, the US Air Force had 1124 F-16s in service, including those assigned to the Air National Guard and the US Air Force Reserve. Air Force units included Tactical Fighter Squadrons of the Tactical Air Command, the Pacific Air Forces and the US Air Forces in Europe, as well as the Air Force Thunderbirds aerobatic demonstration team. These aircraft were only a part of the 3047 that the Air Force had planned to acquire through fiscal year 1994.

The Falcon is the most successful major export fighter in years. In addition to those in service with the US Air Force, over 400 are also in service in Belgium, Denmark, the Netherlands and Norway, which were the original participating countries, as well as many others (*see chart*) including the air forces of six additional countries and the air arm of the US Navy, which would be using the small and maneuverable Falcon under the F-16N designation for aggressor training in its Top Gun exercises. Being dissimilar in appearance to familiar Navy aircraft, the F-16N would be used to simulate Soviet bloc tactics in mock air battles with regular Navy units. The decision of the Navy to buy a plane named after the Air Force Academy mascot marked the first time that the Navy had purchased a major first-line jet that was already in service with the Air Force. It was also the first time since the Air Force went for the Navy's F-4 Phantom that the two services would be using the same type of major high performance fighter.

F-16 Program Status	Delivered Through October 1987	Total Contracted through October 1987	First Operational Acquisition
US Air Force	1209 *	1859	1979
US Navy	15	26	1987
Belgium	116	160	1979
Denmark	58	70	1980
The Netherlands	161	214	1979
Norway	72	72	1980
Israel	124	150	1981
Egypt	80	120	1982
Pakistan	40	40	1982
Venezuela	24	24	1983
Korea	21	36	1986
Turkey		160	1987
Greece		40	
Thailand		12	
Singapore		8	
Indonesia		(not specified)	
Bahrain		12	
Totals	1920	3003	

*US Air Force total excludes eight prototype and development aircraft and two F-16XLs currently in storage.

F-16C Falcon
(advanced version of F-16A)

F-16F Falcon
(based on F-16XL prototype)

F-16D Falcon
(two-seat version of F-16C)

Above: Two Hill AFB-based F-16 Fighting Falcons bank left over the Utah countryside. Note the Sidewinders on their wingtips, and the bombs on underwing pylons. *Below:* An F-16 in flight over the Nevada desert in 1979. In addition to the F-16s it now flies, the USAF also evaluated, but lacked funding for, the delta-wing F-16F—of which two prototypes are currently in storage at General Dynamics. *Below opposite,* left and right: Views of the conventional F-16 and the delta-wing (low drag, high lift) F-16F.

As we have noted, the McDonnell Douglas F/A-18 Hornet evolved out of the Northrop YF-17 program that was evaluated against the F-16. This involved a McDonnell Douglas-Northrop collaboration to meet the US Navy's need for a lightweight fighter-bomber. Because the Hornet would fly with both fighter (VF) *and* attack (VA) squadrons, it was designated both as F-18 and as A-18, hence the F/A-18 designation.

The first flight of a Hornet occurred in November 1978, with the first carrier trials taking place aboard the USS *America* in October 1979. The aircraft entered squadron service with the Navy's FA-125 (*Rough Riders*) at Lemoore NAS, California in November 1980 and with the Marine Corps' VMFA-314 at El Toro MCAS, California the following year.

Selected as the next generation fighter by the air forces of Canada and Australia, it was first delivered to those services in 1983 and 1985. (Australian pilots began F/A-18 training in the United States with Australian-owned Hornets in 1984, but the first deliveries 'down under' were made by RAAF pilots in May 1985.) Ultimately, the US Navy and Marine Corps will take delivery of over 1300 F/A-18s while the Canadian Armed Forces Air Command will buy 138, the Royal Australian Air Force 75 (most of them built in Australia) and Spain will order at least 72.

Above: A McDonnell Douglas F/A-18 Hornet set up for reconnaissance duty rolls out above the broad ocean. Note the camera ports just behind its nose. *At right:* Three US Marine Corps Hornets. *Below:* F/A-18 Hornets ready on the carrier USS *Constellation's* catapults.

Tactical Combat Aircraft of the 1980s

Specifications	Grumman F-14 Tomcat	McDonnell Douglas F-15 Eagle	General Dynamics F-16 Falcon	McDonnell Douglas F/A-18 Hornet	McDonnell Douglas AV-8B Harrier	Fairchild Republic A-10
First Flight	1970	1972	1974	1978	1978	1972
US user service(s)	US Navy	US Air Force	US Air Force US Navy	US Navy US Marine Corps	US Marine Corps	US Air Force
Function	Fighter	Fighter/ Fighter Bomber	Fighter/ Fighter Bomber	Fighter Bomber/ Ground Attack	Ground Attack	Ground Attack
Wing span	62'2"(spread) 38'2"(swept)	42'10"	32'10"	40'8"	30'4"	57'6"
Length	61'11"	63'9"	49'4"	56'	46'4"	53'4"
Gross weight	73,248 lb	68,000 lb	37,500 lb	33,580 lb	29,750 lb	40,269 lb
Top speed	Mach 2.3	Mach 2.5	Mach 2	Mach 1.8	Mach 1.1	460 mph
Range	2000 mi	3400 mi	2300 mi	2300 mi	2000 mi	3510 mi
Engine	Pratt & Whitney TF30 turbofans (2)	Pratt & Whitney F100 turbofans (2)	Pratt & Whitney F100 turbofans (1)	General Electric F404 turbofans (2)	Rolls Royce Pegasus 105 (1)	General Electric TF34 (2)
Engine thrust	20,900 lb	23,930 lb	25,000 lb	16,000 lb	21,750 lb	9065 lb

* First flights are for series prototype, other data is for F-14A, F-15C, F-16C, F/A-18, AV-8B (preceded by British Aerospace AV-8A) and A-10A.

Above: The easily-identifiable Boeing E-3A Sentry AWACS (Airborne Warning and Control System) is the predominate airborne early warning and battle management aircraft of the Western World. *Below:* A radar operator aboard an E-3A views his craft's theater of operations for potential 'bogeys.' The E-3A is based on the airframe of Boeing's familiar Model 707, and is similar to the KC-135 (Model 717). *Below right:* The jet that can out-maneuver anything, the heavily-armed AV-8B Harrier II. The Harrier is a favorite with the US Marine Corps. McDonnell Douglas makes the hoverable, vertical-liftoff AV-8 in association with British Aerospace. *Above right:* The Fairchild Republic A-10 Thunderbolt, aka the 'Warthog,' is a tough, maneuverable and reliable tank-buster with a huge GAU-8A cannon and vast underwing ordnance capacity.

Since the B-52 began to replace the B-36 as SAC's leading heavy bomber after it had been in service for less than ten years, the search for a successor to the B-52 began in the 1950s. The XB-70 program came and went as a possibility and studies continued. A number of proposals were considered under the Advanced Manned Strategic Aircraft (AMSA) project in the 1960s before the US Air Force finally, in June 1970, settled on North American (since 1967 a division of Rockwell International) to build the new bomber.

Designated B-1, it first flew on 23 December 1974. A second prototype flew in June 1976. However, in June 1977, newly-elected President Jimmy Carter made good on his campaign pledge to cancel the program. The Carter administration did, however, permit completion of two additional prototypes and the continuation of a flight test program. In 1981, when the Carter administration was replaced by that of Ronald Reagan, the need to begin replacing the aging B-52 fleet in SAC's front line had become critical.

In October 1981, the Reagan administration decided that the best way to address this requirement would be with an upgraded B-1 that would take advantage of the original design and the years of flight testing. Rockwell International was given a contract to build 100 new bombers under the designation B-1B and two of the original aircraft were modified to B-1B standards so that flight testing could begin as early as 1983.

Outwardly similar to the original B-1A except for greatly redesigned engine nacelles, the first all-new B-1B rolled out in September 1984. The redesign of the nacelles made the B-1B a slower-cruising aircraft, but this was just one of a number of new features that made the new plane appear a tenth the size of the B-1A on radar scopes. Avionics systems were also a decade newer and the bomb load was increased.

The first B-1B joined the Strategic Air Command in June 1985, the first new strategic bomber to enter service outside the Soviet Union in a quarter century. By June 1986, the first anniversary of the B-1Bs arrival at SAC's Dyess AFB, 15 aircraft had been delivered to the Air Force. By 1 October when the 96th Bombardment Wing reached its Initial Operating Capacity (IOC) with the new bomber, 23 had been produced, and by 21 January 1987 when the first B-1B was delivered to Ellsworth AFB, South Dakota, the total produced had reached 36. After having delivered only four aircraft during 1985, Rockwell reached a point in December 1986 after which it would produce no fewer than

four a *month*. Meanwhile, the 4018th Combat Crew Training Squadron at Dyess was turning out the crews to man the big planes.

On 14 April 1987, a Dyess-based B-1B took off on a 21 hour, 40 minute nonstop demonstration of the bomber's endurance capability. Taking off at a gross weight of 413,000 pounds—73,000 pounds above normal for operational training missions—the aircraft covered 9411 miles on a course that took it across Alaska to within 160 nautical miles of the Soviet Union.

By the time that a B-1B was ready to go on display at the Paris Air Show in June 1987, Rockwell's four-a-month delivery schedule had put more than half the original order of 100 bombers into the Air Force inventory. Dyess AFB had reached IOC with 15 aircraft in September 1986 and had its full complement of B-1Bs by December. Having received its first bomber in January 1987, Ellsworth AFB received its 35th, and last, in September. Grand Forks AFB, North Dakota received its 17th, and last, B-1B in December as deliveries began to McConnell AFB, Kansas. The final delivery, scheduled for mid-1988, proceeded ahead of schedule with check-out time reduced to 15 days per aircraft. As the US Air Force's Strategic Air Command put the final production B-1B into service in 1988, it marked 31 years since the inception of the B-70 program, the original heavy bomber replacement for the B-52. It had been 18 years since the inception of the original B-1 program, yet only six years since the B-1B program had been given the go-ahead. Thanks in part to the B-1A tests between 1974 and 1982, it had taken less time to build 100 B-1Bs than it had to build the original four B-1A prototypes.

	B-1A	**B-1B**
Wing span (spread)	136'8.5"	135'8.5"
(swept)	75'2.5"	78'2.5"
Length	150'2.5"	147'0"
Gross weight	389,000 lb	477,000 lb
Top speed	Mach 2.1 at Altitude	Mach 1 at Altitude
Range	6100 mi	6200+ mi
Engine	General Electric F-101-GE-100	General Electric F-101-GE-102
Engine thrust	30,000 lb	30,000 lb

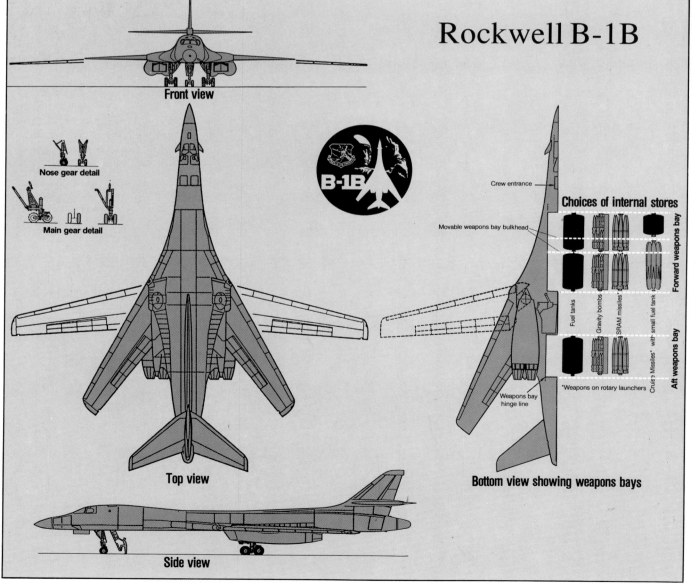

Rockwell B-1B

Front view

Nose gear detail

Main gear detail

Top view

Side view

Crew entrance

Choices of internal stores

Movable weapons bay bulkhead

Fuel tanks — Gravity bombs — SRAM missiles — Cruise Missiles* with small fuel tank

Forward weapons bay

Aft weapons bay

*Weapons on rotary launchers

Weapons bay hinge line

Bottom view showing weapons bays

This bomber is slated to replace the USAF's legendary B-52. *Above:* The Rockwell variable wing-sweep B-1 bomber in flight. The B-1B is a slower, but more capacious, longer-range and much more radar-slippery bird than the prototypical B-1A was. *Below:* The B-1B *Star of Abilene* undergoes an avionics checkout at Rockwell's Palmdale, California factory, across the runway from Lockheed's top-secret 'Skunk Works' facility. This particular B-1B is assigned to the SAC 96th Bomb Wing at Dyess AFB in Abilene, Texas.

The bulk of the airlift operations carried out by the US Air Force Military Airlift Command (MAC) is handled by a family of three types of Lockheed transports with distinctly different, yet complementary, size and weight characteristics. One might go so far as to characterize them as 'medium' (the C-130 Hercules), 'large' (the C-141 Starlifter) and 'extra-large' (the C-5 Galaxy).

The C-130 Hercules entered operational service in 1956 and has become, during its three decades, the real workhorse of American Military Airlift. It has served everywhere in the world where the US Air Force, the Air Force Reserve or the Air Guard are active, from Europe to Antarctica, and in a wide variety of roles. Basically, the turboprop-powered Hercules is an intra-theater tactical airlifter; it is also used as a paratroop plane, as an air ambulance or a long-range transport. C-130s have been modified to fight forest fires and for air-snatch recovery of satellites and reconnaissance drones.

The MC-130 has been outfitted with *Combat Talon* equipment to recover objects or persons from the ground by cable in a low-level pass. It is equipped with terrain-following radar, precision navigation, airdrop avionics and in-flight refueling capability. The AC-130 Spectre Gunship is one of the most heavily armed aircraft in the Air Force. The HC-130 is the principal fixed-wing aircraft in service with the ARRS and Air Guard and Reserve Rescue Squadrons. The WC-130 is equipped for weather reconnaissance, including penetration of tropical storms to obtain data for forecasting storm movements.

Lockheed C-130 (Military) Hercules

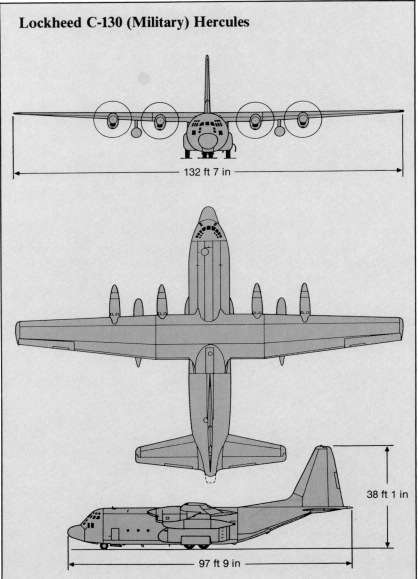

Commercial Hercules (L-100)

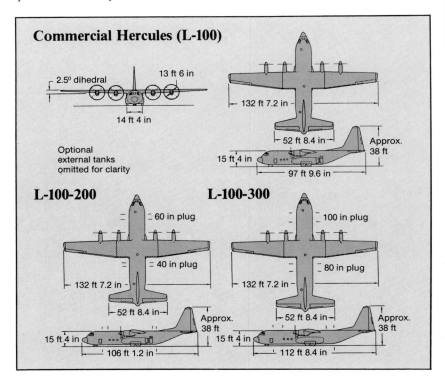

Above: The Lockheed C-130 Hercules, the workhorse of the American military airlift. The C-130 is still in production with over 1600 military versions built between 1954 and 1987. The four largest orders came from the US Air Force and included 188 C-130As, 118 C-130Bs, 389 C-130Es and 136 C-130Hs; meanwhile, deliveries of the civil version (*left*) through 1986 included 22 L-100s, 27 L-100-20s and 58 L-100-30s. *Below:* A Military Airlift Command 'Herc' being positioned on an airfield in one of its many global theaters of operation. *At right:* The versatile Hercules here appears as a US Coast Guard HC-130H long range surveillance aircraft. Hercules have also been outfitted as Lockheed's own High Technology Test Bed (HTTB), and as the AC-130 Spectre heavy gun platform.

Military Transports of the 1980s

Specifications[*]	Lockheed C-130 Hercules	Lockheed C-141 Starlifter	Lockheed C-5 Galaxy	Boeing VC-137	McDonnell Douglas C-9 Nightingale
First Flight[*]	1954	1965	1968	**	**
Wing span	132'7"	159'11"	222'9"	145'9"	93'5"
Length	97'9"	168'3.5"	247'10"	152'11"	119'4"
Gross weight	175,000 lb	343,000 lb	769,000 lb	322,000 lb	108,000 lb
Cruising speed	300 mph	566 mph	571 mph	627 mph	565 mph
Range	840 mi	2293 mi	2729 mi	5150 mi	2000 mi
Engine	Allison T-56 turboprops (4)	Pratt & Whitney TF-33 turbofans (4)	General Electric TF-39 turbofans (4)	Pratt & Whitney JT3D turbofans (4)	Pratt & Whitney JT8D turbofans (2)
Engine rating	4508 hp	21,000 lb thrust	43,000 lb thrust	18,000 lb thrust	14,500 lb thrust

*   First flights are for series prototypes (except VC-137 and C-9), data is for C-130E, C-141B, C-5A, VC-137C and C-9A.

** VC-137 and C-9 are commercial Model 707 and DC-9 aircraft specially adapted as VIP transport and aeromedical airlifter respectively.

The C-141 Starlifter is the next size up from the C-130 and is also in service with MAC around the world as both transport and paratroop planes supporting Army and Air Force activities. The C-141A became operational in April 1965 and immediately began daily supply missions to Southeast Asia. After a decade in service, the entire fleet of C-141s went back to Lockheed for modification as C-141Bs. This involved making the planes aerial-refuelable, which lengthened the fuselage by 15 feet. The C-130 carries six standard 463L cargo pallets (the C-141A would carry ten); now the C-141B carries thirteen. Modification of the fleet of 270 aircraft is equivalent to building 90 new C-141As. The first C-141B flew in 1977, with the last completed and put into squadron service in 1982. Like the smaller C-130 and larger C-5, the C-141 has the wing mounted high on the fuselage to minimize cabin obstruction and to give the planes more clearance when operating from rough, remote landing fields.

The C-5 Galaxy is the largest plane of any type in service in the world, carrying 36 of the standard 463L pallets in a cargo hold that reminds one of a gymnasium interior. The payload of these turbofan-powered monsters exceeds 100 tons, which translates as two Army M-60 main battle tanks or three CH-47 helicopters. With aerial refueling, the C-5 gives MAC the ability to move any item of equipment in the Army's arsenal anywhere in the world in a matter of hours. The first C-5A became operational with MAC in December 1969, with all 81 delivered by May 1973. Like the smaller airlifters, the C-5 provides airlift support for Army and Air Force activities and readiness exercises worldwide. Though only 77 are now in service, their enormous size makes their presence felt. In 1980 the C-5As began to undergo wing strengthening modifications to extend their service life to 30,000 hours. In 1984, the Air Force accepted the first of 50 all-new C-5Bs.

In addition to its airlift duties, MAC is also in the executive transportation business. Five Boeing VC-137s (the VIP version of the basic Model 707 jetliner) of the 89th MAW, including *Air Force One*, and over one hundred Rockwell CT-39 Sabreliners—small, four-to seven-passenger executive jets used for shuttling small numbers of personnel between bases—are MAC's most important executive transports. The CT-39s are a basic utility aircraft and virtually identical to the commercial Sabreliner. As the *T* prefix indicates, the Air Force uses the Sabreliners for training as well as transport. While most of the USAF Sabreliners are in service with MAC, a few are the PACAF, AFSC and AFCC. The balance of MAC's fixed-wing fleet includes such other light executive transports as the Lockheed Jetstar (Air Force designation C-140), the Beechcraft Super King (Air Force designation C-12) and finally the McDonnell Douglas C-9.

The C-9 is the military version of the standard McDonnell Douglas DC-9 commercial jetliner, converted for use as an aeromedical airlift transport, or air ambulance. They serve the Air Force as the C-9A Nightingale and the US Navy as the C-9B Skytrain II. The C-9A became operational with the Air Force in August 1968, with delivery of 21 of them to MAC's 375th Aeromedical Airlift Wing at Scott AFB completed in February 1973. Most are still based at Scott, but three are assigned to Clark AB in the Pacific and three to Rhein-Main AB in Europe. Among the facilities aboard the C-9 are refrigeration; a medical supply work area; oxygen system; a hydraulic folding ramp for efficient loading of stretchers and supplies; a special ventilation system for isolating an intensive care section; and provision for electrical power for cardiac monitors, respirators, incubators and infusion pumps at any location in the cabin. The Nightingale's interior configuration is easily modified to accept various combinations of stretcher or ambulatory patients. The C-9 fleet flies over 3000 missions annually, airlifting over 60,000 patients. The US Navy version is designated C-9B.

Below: Lockheed C-5A Galaxies of the 60th Military Airlift Wing line up on the flight line at Travis Air Force Base. Even a medium battle tank would be overwhelmed by the size of the surroundings here, as is the ground equipment truck in this photo. Between the US military's medium C-130 transport and the *extra*-large C-5 transport lies the US military's simply *large* transport, the Lockheed C-141 Starlifter, which has a payload capacity of 90,200 pounds. In the photo *at below left* are, at front, a C-141B and at rear, a C-141A.

Lockheed C-5 Galaxy

Above: A C-5B Galaxy takes to the air in that model's 'European I' camouflage paint scheme. Despite its monumental bulk, the Galaxy flies as sweet as (an awfully large) canary. Test pilot Bernie Dvorscak, the first to take the controls of the improved C-5B version, said, 'It does everything it's supposed to do. The first flight went so well, we extended it by an hour.' Also despite its giant dimensions, the C-5 takes off and lands in an area comparable to today's commercial airliners. In a 1972 demonstration, a 40-ton Minuteman missile was *successfully air-launched* from a C-5A! On 17 December 1984, a C-5A carrying a 116-ton payload was flown at a gross weight of 922,000 pounds—the heaviest weight at which any aircraft has ever flown.

At left: A sectional view showing the C-5 Galaxy's upper deck crew space and galley, and its cavernous 13.5-foot high by 19-foot wide by 144.6-foot deep front-and-rear access cargo hold.

Because the US Air Force Strategic Air Command (SAC) has responsibility for carrying out the nation's strategic war plan, it is also charged with planning. Since planning requires information, SAC operates for the Air Force a fleet of the most sophisticated reconnaissance aircraft in the world. The Lockheed U-2, designed for very high altitude reconnaissance, was introduced secretly in the 1950s and used to monitor ICBM sites within the Soviet Union—until one piloted by Francis Gary Powers was brought down by a Russian SAM over Sverdlovsk in 1960, creating an international incident. The early U-2s remained an important part of the USAF reconnaissance arsenal through the 1960s and 1970s over Cuba, Vietnam and other trouble spots. The basic U-2A and B have been modified into such diverse types as the electronic patrol version designated U-2EPX and the weather reconnaissance aircraft, the TR-1, which first flew in 1981. The TR-1, like the U-2R, has a 103-foot wingspan and operates at extremely high altitudes, equipped with cameras and sensors for day or night all-weather reconnaissance.

The SR-71 Blackbird, another Lockheed product, is a unique aircraft of extremely high performance. Designed in the 1960s, it incorporates technology that is not known to have been equaled or surpassed since. Wearing flight suits made from the same mold as the lunar mission and Space Shuttle suits, the SR-71 pilots take their aircraft to the edge of space, to over 100,000 feet, at speeds well in excess of Mach 3. The SR-71 combines a unique fuselage and wing contour and enormously powerful engines to achieve speeds that no other aircraft has been able to touch since the Blackbird set the World's Absolute Speed record of 2193.167 mph in July 1976. As the pilot says about his amazing plane, 'The real beauty is in what you can't and will never see.' He is referring to the extremely sensitive electronic and photographic gear within the SR-71: its sophisticated battlefield surveillance systems have the capability of covering 100,000 square miles in a single hour.

The spy planes: The Lockheed SR-71 Blackbird *(at right)* has flown to the edge of space, and with only *partial throttle* has attained speeds faster than 2100 mph. *Above:* A TR-1 jockey and his steed. *Below:* A U-2 such as Francis Gary Powers flew in 1960.

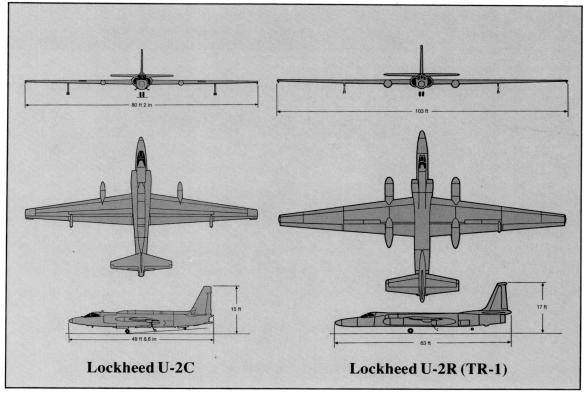

Lockheed U-2C

Lockheed U-2R (TR-1)

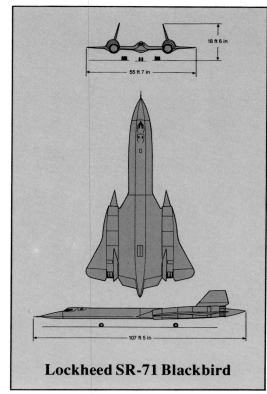

Lockheed SR-71 Blackbird

Evolution of the US National Insignia

1906-1916
Used with and without white background circle. In use at the time of the Mexican Border Campaign.

1918-1920
The official American insignia during World War I. It began to be phased out in 1919.

1917, 1921-1941
Introduced prior to the American entry into World War I and officially readopted after the war.

1942-1943
The red center of the 1921-1941 insignia was removed unofficially in December 1941 and officially in May 1942 to avoid confusion with Japanese insignia.

1942-1943
Some aircraft in the European and Mediterranean theaters unofficially incorporated a yellow surround in the British style.

1943
Between 29 June and 14 August, the official national insignia incorporated white sidebars and an overall red surround.

1943-1947
The red surround of the official insignia was quickly changed to a *blue* surround. During its four years of use, this insignia appeared on more aircraft than all its predecessors combined.

1947-Present
With the reorganization of the Defense Department and the creation of the USAF, red bars were added to the official national insignia. A variation of this insignia appears officially without the blue surround on F-15 aircraft.

Low Visibility

Beginning in the late seventies low visibility markings have been introduced officially and unofficially on the aircraft of the USAF and other services. The grey insignia on the far left is the only insignia used on operational F-16s. It is followed by a more standard low visibility mark, used on A-10s and other aircraft. The stencil marks are becoming increasingly common on MAC, AFRES and Air National Guard aircraft.

Major USAAF/USAF Bombers
and their Periods of Service

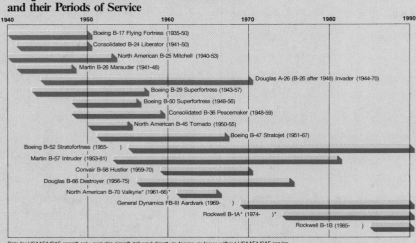

Data for USAAF/USAF aircraft only, excludes aircraft delivered directly to foreign air forces without USAAF/USAF service.
Periods begin with operational service, not first recorded flight. Periods include service with Air National Guard, but do not include mothballed aircraft.
*Neither the B-70 nor B-1A were production aircraft. Data for them is given only as a point of interest.

Major USAAF/USAF Bombers
Total Number Delivered

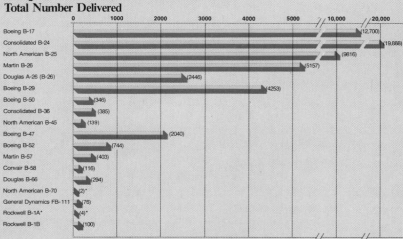

Major USAAF/USAF Cargo Aircraft
and their Periods of Service

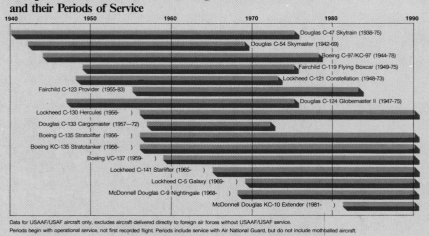

Data for USAAF/USAF aircraft only, excludes aircraft delivered directly to foreign air forces without USAAF/USAF service.
Periods begin with operational service, not first recorded flight. Periods include service with Air National Guard, but do not include mothballed aircraft.

Major USAAF/USAF Cargo Aircraft
Total Number Delivered

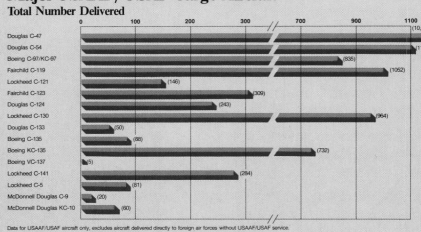

Data for USAAF/USAF aircraft only, excludes aircraft delivered directly to foreign air forces without USAAF/USAF service.

The charts on the *lower halves* of these pages cover US Air Force aircraft, and the photo *above* shows a collection of current US Navy/US Marine Corps aircraft; from the front in the front row are: The McDonnell Douglas F/A-18 Hornet, with over 1300 units in USN/USMC service starting in 1978; the McDonnell Douglas AV-8B Harrier II, with nearly 100 units in USMC service since 1984; the Douglas A-4 Skyhawk, of which over 2519 were built for the USN and USMC from 1954–1979; two Vought A-7 Corsair IIs (both single and two-seat versions), of which over 1000 have been built for the USN since 1965; the Grumman A-6 Intruder, of which nearly 800 have seen service since 1960; the McDonnell Douglas F-4 Phantom II, of which 1208 were built for the USN and USMC after 1955; and the Grumman F-14 Tomcat, with over 300 units in service starting in 1970. From the front in the back row are: the Douglas KA-3 Skywarrior, with 282 units built for the USN starting in 1952; the Lockheed S-3 Viking, of which 179 were built for the USN from 1972-1978; and two Lockheed P-3 Orions, of which over 500 have been built for the Navy. The photo was taken at the Naval Air Test Center at Patuxent River NAS, Maryland.

Major USAAF/USAF Fighters
and their Periods of Service

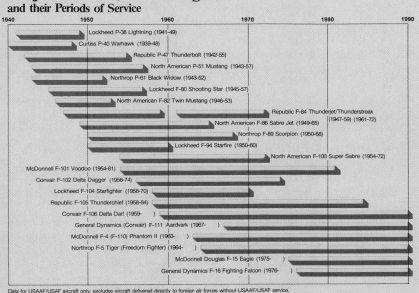

Data for USAAF/USAF aircraft only, excludes aircraft delivered directly to foreign air forces without USAAF/USAF service.
Periods begin with operational service, not first recorded flight. Periods include service with Air National Guard, but do not include mothballed aircraft.

Major USAAF/USAF Fighters
Total Number Delivered

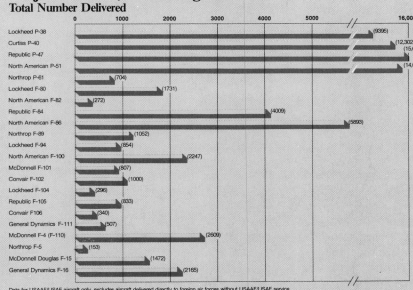

Data for USAAF/USAF aircraft only, excludes aircraft delivered directly to foreign air forces without USAAF/USAF service.

Major USAAF/USAF Attack Aircraft
and their Periods of Service

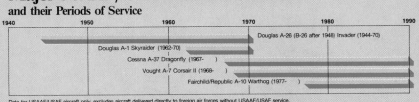

Data for USAAF/USAF aircraft only, excludes aircraft delivered directly to foreign air forces without USAAF/USAF service.
Periods begin with operational service, not first recorded flight. Periods include service with Air National Guard, but do not include mothballed aircraft.

Major USAAF/USAF Attack Aircraft
Total Number Delivered

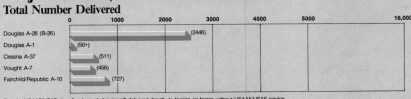

Data for USAAF/USAF aircraft only, excludes aircraft delivered directly to foreign air forces without USAAF/USAF service.

AMERICAN COMMERCIAL AIRCRAFT TODAY

The spectrum of American commercial aircraft in service throughout the world in the 1980s is firmly grounded in the jetliner boom of the 1960s. All of the Boeing and Douglas jetliners are still in service, as is the Lockheed L-1011 TriStar. However, the L-1011 is no longer in production, nor is the DC-8 or the Boeing 727. Only two all-new American jetliners have made their debut since the L-1011 and DC-10 joint arrival in 1970. The manufacturer of these two all-new jetliners not only has emerged as the leader in the American, as well as world, jetliner business, but its name has become the word which defines that business: Boeing.

The Boeing 757 and 767, first flown in January 1982 and September 1981, respectively, expanded the product line of the Seattle planemaker to allow it to compete effectively with any segment of the market. Domestic competition for Boeing has narrowed dramatically. Lockheed has left the jetliner business, while McDonnell Douglas has reduced its product line to the MD-80 (the redesignated DC-9-80), and an occasional DC-10. An improved DC-10, designated MD-11, is envisioned for possible development in the 1990s.

Boeing's major competition today comes from Airbus Industrie, the international consortium based in Toulouse, France, which is seriously developing its own 'family' of jetliners, but which is still far behind Boeing's lead.

Boeing's product line today includes all the familiar jetliners, although the 707 is available only in specialized versions. The most popular is the little 737, followed by the huge 747 at the other end of the size range. Both of these aircraft have evolved over the years, with the turbofan-powered 737-300 now replacing the older 737-200 turbojet. In September 1982, the extended upper deck version of the 747, designated 747-300, was introduced. The extended upper deck permitted a much greater passenger load than had ever been possible on an airliner before. In October 1985, Boeing announced its 747-400, an updated version of the 747-300 that offered greater fuel economy

continued on page 198

Below: **Boeing's short-to medium-range jetliner, the Model 757 is a handy complement to the longer-range Boeing 767. Even though Lockheed and McDonnell Douglas have essentially left the airliner field to Boeing, McDonnell Douglas still makes the MD-80 *(at right).***

and greater range.

As of June 1987, Boeing had delivered 5196 jetliners against orders for 5944, giving its factories a backlog of 748 aircraft. Of the aircraft already delivered, 35 percent were 727s, 27 percent were 737s and 19 percent were 707s. Of the future orders, 58 percent were 737s, 16 percent were 747s (including 747-200s) and the balance was divided between 757s and 767s, with a handful of 707s still on the factory floor.

Although Boeing has given the United States the undisputed lead in large commercial aircraft, the field of smaller general aviation aircraft contains a number of important international contenders such as British Aerospace (UK), Canadair (Canada), Dassault-Breguet (France), Israel Aircraft (Israel), and Fokker (the Netherlands), to name just a few.

Among the most important American manufacturers of light planes are Beech Aircraft (Beechcraft), whose product line includes the Beechjet, King Air and Super King Air; Cessna Aircraft, whose products include the Citation, Caravan and Conquest; Gates Learjet; Gulfstream; Lear Fan; Sabreliner and Piper Aircraft, whose Cheyenne is only just the latest in a long line of aircraft, including the Cub, developed by the company that William T Piper bought for $1000 back in 1931. Currently Cessna is the largest general aviation manufacturer in the United States.

At top, above: The Boeing 757 (background) and the 767, which designs gave Boeing a complete size range of airliners. *Above:* A typical flight deck aboard either of Boeing's two intermediate airliners, the 757 or 767. *At right:* A Delta Airlines Boeing 767 overflies the Rocky Mountains. The 767 variants include the extended-range (5600-mile) 767-200ER.

Jetliners of the 1980s

Specifications	Boeing 767	Boeing 757	McDonnell Douglas MD-80*	Boeing 747-300	Boeing 747-400
First Flight	1981	1982	1983	1982	1988
Wing span	156′1″	124′6″	107′10″	212′2″	212′2″
Length	159′2″	155′3″	147′10″	231′10″	231′10″
Gross weight	310,000 lb	220,000 lb	140,000 lb	800,000 lb	850,000 lb
Cruising speed	600 mph	600 mph	542 mph	600 mph	600 mph
Range	3746 mi	2867 mi	2071 mi	7165 mi	8100 mi
Engine	(two turbofans) customer choice of a. Pratt & Whitney JT9D b. General Electric CF-6	(two turbofans) customer choice of a. Pratt & Whitney PW2037 b. Rolls Royce RB211	(two turbofans) Pratt & Whitney JT8D	(four turbofans) customer choice of a. Pratt & Whitney PW4256 b. General Electric CF-6 c. Rolls Royce RB211	(four turbofans) customer choice of a. Pratt & Whitney PW4256 b. General Electric CF-6 c. Rolls Royce RB211
Engine thrust	a. 47,800 lb b. 48,000 lb	a. 38,200 lb b. 37,400 lb	18,500 lb	50,000 lb (nominal)	56,000 lb (nominal)

* The type originally flew in 1979 as the DC-9 series 80, a stretched version of the DC-9. It was redesignated under the new McDonnell Douglas nomenclature in 1983.

Above: One up on the standard Boeing 747 super-jetliner, the Boeing 747-400 is the only 747 configuration that has stabilizing winglets and shares the 280-inch extended upper deck which previously appeared only on the 747-300. It has been said that the Boeing 767 is the company's 'flagship of the eighties,' even as the phenomenal 747 was Boeing's 'flagship of the seventies'—if so, the 767 must prove to be a worthy flagship indeed. *Below:* The flight deck of the Boeing 747-300, which seems a small control room for such a large and sophisticated aircraft; but—as some might say even when discussing that which is superbly functional—'It sure gets the job done!'

Despite their excellent Cheyenne 400LS *(immediately above)*, a 400+ mph propjet that can fly at 41,000 feet, Piper is planning to boost business with a revival of the ever-popular Cub *(see page 82)*, and with a host of new designs—under the leadership of Stuart Millar.

The multiseat Beechcraft Baron 58 *(at top, above)* cruises at 233 mph. *Above opposite:* The 400 mph+ Beechcraft propjet Starship 1 was designed by Burt Rutan, who is discussed in the following chapter. Beechcraft, too, suffers in the current business climate.

Despite a drop in overall American private plane production from 17,811 units to 1100 units spanning the years 1978–1987, such well-known business jets as the Gates Learjet continue in production. Pictured *at right* is a Learjet Model 55C.

Cessna, the largest builder of general aviation aircraft in the United States, temporarily suspended its piston-engine lines in 1986 in favor of its Citation family of business jets, pending a more solid demand base in the near future. *At top, above:* The Citation I, which design gave rise to the more powerful Citation II *(at right)*, which itself has led to the larger Citation III *(above)*, with a completely redesigned wing.

THE RUTAN BROTHERS AND THE *VOYAGER*

Like the story of the brothers Wright, with whom this book begins, the story of *Voyager* involves two brothers, each with a unique commitment to ideals of aircraft design and airmanship. Dick Rutan and Jeana Yeager took *Voyager* to its unique place in history by being the first people to circumnavigate the globe nonstop without refueling in December 1986. Burt Rutan, meanwhile, will be remembered as the man who conceived and designed the extraordinary *Voyager*, an airplane like no other which had ever flown.

Burt Rutan, who must be considered one of the most innovative aircraft designers in the world today, began his career designing and flying radio-controlled models in the 1950s when he was just a boy. Having graduated from California Polytechnic in San Luis Obispo, Rutan went to Kansas to work for Jim Bede on the latter's BD-5. Still dreaming of one day building an airplane of his own design, Rutan returned to California where his first VariViggen flew in 1972. A tiny delta-winged craft with a canard foreplane, VariViggen was designed so that a hobbyist could buy it in kit form, take it home, put it together and fly away. Two years after its first flight, VariViggen was named Outstanding New Design by the Experimental Aircraft Association!

Orders for VariViggen kits helped to establish Burt's Rutan Aircraft Factory at Mojave Airport in California's high desert. The second Rutan creation, the VariEze, first flew in 1975 with Burt's brother Dick as test pilot. The reputation of the Rutan Aircraft Factory grew throughout the late seventies as several new designs were introduced and marketed. In the meantime, Burt Rutan designed his Model 35, a high-wing monoplane whose long, straight wing rotated *in-flight* to a position almost parallel. The Model 35 became NASA's AD-1 research plane and Rutan went on to design his pusher-engined, canard Model 115 which became the Beech Starship.

By the early 1980s, Burt Rutan was ready to design and build an airplane which, like the Wright Flyer so long before it, was considered theoretically impossible. Burt Rutan had decided to build an airplane that could fly around the world nonstop. Several times since World War II, strategic bombers had done this, but it had required several in-flight refuelings, and it was generally accepted that for a plane to do it *without* in-flight refueling would require it to carry so much fuel that it would be too heavy to get off the ground!

Through the use of lightweight composite materials, with which he had already developed an expertise, Burt Rutan was sure he could do it. Dick Rutan had already established numerous new size and weight class distance and endurance records in Burt's aircraft. He had, for example, flown Burt's LongEze from Anchorage, Alaska 4563 miles to the West Indies in 1981.

In that same year Burt began the first work on the twin-engined *Voyager*, a wispy, broad-winged one-of-a-kind craft designed to carry more than twice its own weight in fuel. It was designed to accommodate two pilots, because an around-the-world flight would take about 250 hours, and Dick Rutan, agreeing with Charles Lindbergh before him, estimated a single pilot's endurance at about 30 hours.

Voyager was hand made at Mojave over a period of about 18 months. The main structure was entirely of lightweight composite—Nomex honeycomb and Kevlar manufactured by Hexall. The engines, donated by Teledyne Continental, were a 1OL-200 aft engine and an O240 forward engine, with propellers donated by TRW/Hartzell. The avionics, custom-configured and donated by King Radio, included a KAP 150 two-axis digital autopilot, a KNS 660 multisensor navigation management with a 4-inch display CRT, a KHF 990 solid-state high-frequency transceiver, a KWX 58 full color weather radar system, a KX 165 VHF radio system, a KI 525A pictorial navigation indicator and a KCS 55A gyrocompass system.

Complete in early 1984, *Voyager* began her taxi and flight test sequence on 22 June. With Dick Rutan and Jeana Yeager at the controls, *Voyager* completed numerous endurance tests over the next two years.

The flight test series culminated with Dick, Jeana and *Voyager* capturing the world record for closed-course distance in July 1986. At 2:52 pm on 10 July they took off from Vandenberg AFB and proceeded to fly an elongated

Above: **A greeting sign on the outskirts of Mojave, California.** *At right:* **Burt Rutan designed it; his brother Dick, and Jeana Yeager, flew it—the distance record holder** *Voyager.*

elliptical closed-course that stretched up the California coast from San Luis Obispo to a point 250 miles north of San Francisco. Five days later, at 6:36 am, they touched down at Mojave, having flown 11,857 miles, 11,600.9 of them within the closed-course. The previous closed-course record, set by a B-52 in 1962, had been 11,336.9 miles. Another B-52 still held the world's *absolute* distance record of 12,532 miles (also set in 1962), but *Voyager* would tackle that one in due course.

When the five day evaluation flight was made, the optimum window for the around-the-world flight was estimated as being between September and November, but the actual takeoff for the flight was pushed back to December.

The takeoff at dawn on 14 December 1986 turned out to be one of the most harrowing moments of the flight. Its wings slumping from the weight of 7001 pounds of fuel, *Voyager* began the takeoff roll on the 15,000 foot Edwards AFB runway only to have the wingtips begin to bang and scrape the asphalt. The winglet on the right wingtip was broken off and 12-18 inches of composite was sheared from the undersides. Nevertheless, Dick Rutan pulled the big bird into the air at 8:02 am and climbed out toward the California coast, with brother Burt hovering nearby in a Beach Duchess chase plane. Burt Rutan examined the wingtips in-flight and diagnosed *Voyager* as fit to continue, provided that the damaged and dangling left winglet didn't peel some skin from the top of the wing when it finally broke. He directed Dick in a right sideslip maneuver that cleanly snapped the winglet off *(see photo, right)*.

Originally planned as a west to east flight, the record attempt was reversed when the original window closed in November, so Rutan and Yeager headed out across the Pacific where they had a day and a half of good flying weather before they encountered typhoon Marge. The storm created severe turbulence which fatigued the crew a great deal and forced them to fly 2000 miles north of the intended flight path. Instead of passing over Australia as planned, they were forced to fly barely 100 miles south of Vietnam. Having cleared Vietnamese airspace on 17 December, they crossed the Malay Peninsula above Kota Bharu and set a course across the Indian Ocean.

Though most of the flight was flown at altitudes of between 7000 and 11,000 feet, thunderstorms encountered as *Voyager* crossed Africa forced the crew to take the plane up to 20,000. Flying any higher would not have been possible due to lack of auxiliary oxygen equipment. Heading out over the Atlantic, *Voyager* picked up a tail wind that pushed its speed to 165 mph and there was guarded optimism until the oil warning light for the aft engine came on. Dick Rutan pumped some extra Mobil synthetic oil into the motor as Yeager flew the plane and monitored the engine's temperature. After this treatment the engine seemed to run fine and the crew continued on toward Brazil and an unexpected storm.

This storm produced the worst turbulence that was encountered on the flight and resulted in the incident that nearly ended the flight in disaster. Dick Rutan had once commented that he never felt comfortable banking the fragile-seeming *Voyager* by more than 15 degrees, but suddenly he felt the craft tossed on its end in a 90 degree bank!

Having righted the plane and restarted his heart, Rutan continued up the east coast of South America toward the Gulf of Mexico and an intended route across Texas. Once more, however, storms lay in wait on the planned path so Yeager and Rutan altered their course and crossed the continent at Costa Rica.

Off the west coast of Mexico the aft engine fuel pump failed and the crew devised a system to bypass it and draw fuel directly from the tank. This worked fine until the night of 22 December when they decided to take *Voyager* down to 8500 feet in search of less headwind. With the plane in a nose-down attitude, the fuel no longer flowed properly and the 1OL-200 sputtered to a stop. The forward engine was not running because it had been standard operating procedure to alternate the engines to conserve fuel. Thus Voyager was briefly a glider until the O240 could be cranked up. Having done this, they restarted the pusher and decided to keep both engines running for the rest of the flight.

At sunrise on the morning of 23 December 1986, *Voyager* made landfall 69 miles south of Long Beach, California, and at 7:35 am it flew over Edwards AFB from whence the flight had started nine days before. Rutan and Yeager made several passes over the field, which was mobbed with well-wishers, before touching down at 8:06 am.

The two crew members struggled out of the incredibly cramped cockpit and sat on the fuselage for several minutes before attempting to walk for the first time in more than a week. They took off with 1192.3 gallons of fuel and returned with 18.3 gallons. Of that, only 9.2 were left in the feed tank. The 25,012 mile flight had been a success and both airplane and engines had functioned in excess of specifications.

Voyager's last flight, 6 January 1987, was a short 18-mile hop to Mojave airport, where the story had begun six years before.

The Rutan*Voyager*	
Wing span	110'10"
Cabin dimensions	7'6"long x 3'4" wide x 3'0" high
Weight	2759 lb (Dry)
	9760 lb (Fully fueled)
Cruising speed	115.8 mph[*]
Range	25,012 mi[**]
Engine manufacturer	Teledyne Continental (Both)
Engine type	Pusher: 1OL-200 (Liquid-cooled)
	Tractor: O240 (Air-cooled)
Engine rating	Pusher: 110 hp
	Tractor: 130 hp

[*] Average speed on the around-the-world flight
[**] Nonstop around-the-world distance record

Index